DEMYSTIFYING BIGOTRY II

Demystifying Bigotry II

The Best of The
America's Race Problem Blog

Paul R. Lehman

Library of Congress Control Number: 2017913819
ISBN: Hardcover   978-1-9845-7422-0
                 Softcover   978-1-9845-7424-4
                 eBook   978-1-9845-7423-7

Print information available on the last page.

Rev. date: 12/26/2018

To order additional copies of this book, contact:
Xlibris
1-888-795-4274
www.Xlibris.com
Orders@Xlibris.com
785191

About the Author

PAUL R. LEHMAN, PhD

Dr. Paul R. Lehman, graduated from Fredrick Douglass High School, Oklahoma City, in 1959, earned a Ph.D. from Lehigh University, 1976. He is a university Professor Emeritus in the department of English, and a former Dean of the Graduate College, at the University of Central Oklahoma, Edmond, Oklahoma. A veteran of the U.S. Navy, he was also a former CBS (affiliate) News Anchor, Journalist, Producer, and Reporter. He is widowed (wife was Marion White) with two adult sons, both with doctoral degrees; his older son Christopher is a professor in Ethnic Studies at St. Cloud State University (MN). His youngest son Jeffrey, a music educator, performer and conductor, is presently living and working in Fairfax, VA.

His teaching experience spans a wide range of subjects including American Literature, Ethnic American Literature, African American Literature, Short Stories, American Fiction, Contemporary Themes as Literature, Chaucer, and English Grammar and Composition.

He has lectured throughout the state of Oklahoma as well as in other states across America. He has published scholarly books, scholarly and creative articles, poetry, short stories, interviews, books, and numerous book reviews. Other recent publications include: *Demystifying Bigotry; The System of European American (white) Supremacy and African American (black) Inferiority; Flannery O'Connor: Southern Racial Culture and African American Characters; America' Race Matters: Returning the Gifts of Race and Color; America's Race Problem: A Practical Guide to Understanding Race in America; The Development of a Black Psyche in the Works of John Oliver Killens; The Making of the Negro in Early American Literature.* He is active in both academic and community service focusing on topics involving cultural biases and implicit biases. Dr. Lehman also writes the blog: americasraceproblems@wordpress.com

CONTACT INFORMATION
www.paulrlehman.com or pmlehman@cox.net or (405) 3418773

Contents

THE BIGGER PICTURE
Part III

Dedicated

To all who help us
See with our heart and our mind
We are all mankind

Foreword

Paul R. Lehman's collection of essays reveals how both terminology and actions hinder equality across ethnic groups. They come from his Wordpress blog *America's Race Problem*, for which he has written throughout the 2010s. In that time he has commented on national ethnic controversies and suggested solutions for those problems. They span the later years of President Barack Obama's administration and the beginning of his successor Donald Trump's inauguration. As various incidents of violence and discrimination against African Americans have taken place over the decade, Lehman has remained steadfast in his beliefs in what is at the root of these actions.

Concerning terminology, usage of the words "race," "racism," and "racist" in discussions about ethnic inequality prolong that inequality. Lehman argues that bigotry--not racism--fuels this inequality. "Race" only scientifically applies to the human race, making inaccurate identification of a group of people according to skin color as a "race." Lehman's writings in Part I warn people that discussing people's skin colors as "races," color-based inequality as "racism," and bigots via skin color as "racists" prolong inequality by validating the inaccurate identification of skin color as "race." He also notes that this central flaw of racism makes any accusation easy for someone accused of racism to refute. For example, the accused can reject being accused of being against a skin-color group by identifying their friends of different colors. "Bigotry" is more precise of a term and one that should replace "racism" in discussions of inequality, as should "bigot" substitute for "racist" and "bigoted" replace "racist."

Police brutality towards African Americans took place during the eras of legal slavery and legal segregation, a. k. a. Jim Crow, and it remains a problem plaguing African Americans nationwide. In Part II Lehman's posts examine the persistence of the criminal justice system's excessive harshness towards African Americans. Some of the writings comment upon the highly publicized shootings of African Americans by police officers. He laments that the constant lack of legal accountability of the officers committing these killings guarantees more of them to follow. To him, bigotry of European Americans leads them to call 911 on innocent African Americans, and it causes judges to convict and sentence African Americans at least partly according to color.

The role of bigotry instead of racism in causing inequality by skin color. The criminal justice system's historic and fundamental inequality will not disappear without a complete overhaul, he argues. Part of this change involves awareness among law enforcement officials of the history of the inequality in their profession. The author also implores people not to call 911 on bigoted impulses based on skin color but rather to take time to critically assess a person's actions. Lehman devotes the third part of the book to his posts that explore solutions to the problems associated with the rhetoric of "race" and the persistence of police brutality. He calls for people to discuss the role of bigotry instead of racism in causing inequality by skin color. The criminal justice system's historic and fundamental inequality will not disappear without a complete overhaul, he argues. Part of this change involves awareness among law enforcement officials of the history of the inequality in their profession. The author also implores people not to call 911 on bigoted impulses based on skin color but rather to take time to critically assess a person's actions.

Christopher P. Lehman,
Professor of Ethnic Studies,
St. Cloud State University,
(son of the author)

Looking Within

Part I

"Real knowledge is to know the extent of one's ignorance."
Confucius

Reflections on Trump's Election and the Challenge for European Americans

November 16, 2018

Much of the trouble today is being caused by changes in our society and the world that people do not understand or appreciate. Many people are concerned and worried about the new president-elect Trump and what effect his presidency will have on society. The people to be most disappointed relative to Trump's election and his presidency will be his base supporters. They will be disappointed because Trump will not be able to deliver on the promises he made during his campaign. Politicians make promises based on things they think their followers want to hear knowing that many of those promises will never be fulfilled. The supporters of many politicians suffer from innocence, ignorance or biases that prevent them from seeing the unrealities of the claims and promises made by their candidate. Once reality sets in, the people will see where they were misled into believing things they wanted to happen were just not possible.

The theme of Trump's campaign was "Make American Great again," which in code language is "make America white again." The phrase and its sentiments have been used time and time again to garner support from the European Americans who believe that they have been left behind by the government in favor of immigrants, women, LGBT, and people of color. They still, however, enjoy the privileges that come with being European American (white) but are in fear of losing them. So, when Trump said that he wanted to make America great again, his followers knew what he meant and felt encouraged that the social changes that had taken place would not threaten their privilege and control. Regardless of what the candidate promised one thing that cannot be stopped is change. Trump supporters called for change, but what they really wanted was no change except to go back to reclaim some of the advantages they believed they lost to immigrants, women, and people of color.

So, what exactly are many European Americans afraid of losing that would cause them to disregard their sense of integrity, character, decency, values, and standards by electing someone who reflects none of these traits? The answer can be found in the social conditioning experienced by Americans since the days of the founding fathers and their inventing and instituting the system of European American (white) supremacy and African American (black) inferiority. In other words, they invented the concept of a black and white race with the white race deemed superior to all non-white races for the purpose of controlling them. Dr. Robin DiAnglo commented on this experience: "This systemic and institutional control allows those of us who are white in North America to live in a social environment that protects and insulates us from race-based stress." She continued by noting that "We have organized society to reproduce and reinforce our racial interests and perspectives. Further, we are centered in all matter deemed normal, universal, benign, neutral and good." With the rapid changes taking place in America, the control presently in the hands of European Americans is under constant threat of change, and is, in fact undergoing change.

The social conditioning European Americans receive in society includes little if any reference to race; therefore, they are never stressful regarding race. Society has told them that they are the representatives of humanity; they are the normal people. All other people belong to a separate race. For example, when stories are reported in the media, usually, the only reference to ethnicity occurs when the subject or subjects of the story are not European American (white). If the story concerns European Americans, ethnicity (race) is never mentioned because society must assume that the subjects are European Americans and no ethnicity (race) is required.

Another feature in American society that conditions the European Americans, as well as the rest of America to the European Americans sense of normalcy can be observed in any pharmacy or department store. All one needs to do is to ask for stockings in a nude or natural color and look closely at the color. The color will match the skin complexion of European Americans. The same scenario exists with cosmetics as well as with bandages and Band-Aids; their color approximates the European Americans' complexion.

European Americans being able to see themselves as normal or without race or ethnic identity is constantly reinforced by and through society. They are also conditioned to see themselves as superior to all other so-called races. Both the elements of normalcy and superiority comes with a large degree of a suspension of disbelief when one realizes that people of color, according to the sciences, were the first of the Homo sapiens to appear on the planet, and in Africa. So, the normal color for a human being would be non-white, not white. Also, the concept of superiority seems questionable in light of the fact that when any person of color procreates with a European American (white), the off spring generally manifest physical characteristics of the parent of color. That would suggest that the superior genes reside within the people of color. In addition, eighty percent of the world's population reflects people of color; that number alone would suggest that the longevity of European Americans (whites) is limited. All those things make little difference when we read that our DNA show we are all from the same family of man and a specific or distinct race cannot be discerned from DNA.

The invention and instituting of the system of European American (white) supremacy and African American (black) inferiority was based on a false concept of race. The fact that the system has been able to sustain itself for so long is due to the control that European Americans have had on society. Now that the system is falling apart due to changes constantly occurring in society, the fear of losing that control and all it represents was possibly at the heart the presidential election. Regardless of who is president, changes will continue to destroy the system of bigotry. The challenge for the European Americans today is replacing the concept of being white and superior with one of being simply a member of the family of mankind without reference to preferences and skin color.

How and Why Bigotry Persist in America

August 14, 2018

An adage frequently heard is "we can't see the forest for the trees," serves as an appropriate description of the problem of bigotry in America. A closer look at how and why bigotry persists in America should give us a better overall perspective.

When the enslaved Africans were brought to America, they were human beings with names, cultures, histories, and languages. Once they arrived, the first order of business for the slave masters and owners was to rid them of the only tangible possessions they had, their names. A person's name is very important because it makes him or her unique, even if the name is the same as other people because each human being is unique. Without a name, we would seemingly not exist simply because no one would know us and so they could not make reference to us because we had no name. So, the first thing the slave masters did was to dehumanize the Africans by taking away their names.

Although a person's name might not seem that important, it is because included in the name is the person's history. When a person's name is taken away, so is his or her history because nothing is available to identify and connect a nameless person with other people. The importance of names and the history they represent are underscored, for example, in the Mexican custom of two given names followed by the father' and mother's name. The person's full name is used, generally, only for legal purposes. Naming children in families after other family members as well as a host of other reasons is common practice today, but when the captured Africans were brought to America, their names were taken away. In place of the names taken, the slaves were renamed by the slave masters, but with only one name. Giving the slaves one name served to prevent them from possessing anything that could be passed along to children. So, a new history was begun for each African captive with the renaming and everything unique and personal relating to their original history was gone. The new names such as slave, negro or black provided no personal identity or significance aside from the connection to the system of American slavery.

The next important element the slave masters and owners took away from the African captives was their language; they were no longer permitted to speak in their native language. The purpose of this action was to prevent the African captives from being able to communicate with fellow countrymen because the ability to communicate with another human being provides a feeling of personal value and worth which also underscores a positive identity. For the slave masters, the process of remaking the African captives could not allow for anything that would give them hope or reference to a former life.

In addition to eliminating the African captives' ability to speak in their native tongue, the slave masters knew that by preventing any reference to their former language the captives would also lose their culture. The culture of a people is embodied in their language, so when the language is removed, so too is the former culture. So, the process of enslavement is not reserved for the physical body, but also to the mind. Unfortunately for the captives, the mind was as important to the slave masters as the body.

When the African captives were enslaved, they lost their physical freedom; they lost their identification; they lost their history, their culture, and their language. They were stripped of everything of value to a human being. The slave masters knowing that they must have complete control of the enslaved immediately began the process of conditioning them to a new world. To begin the process, each slave was shown through brute force and intimidation (chains, shackles, and physical abuse) that they were not free. Then they were given names they had to accept and respond to when ordered, and a new language they must learn. The key element of control was transmitted in and through the slave masters' language.

The primary function of the new language was to inculcate in the minds of the African slaves the system of Anglo-Saxon (white) supremacy. Therefore, as long as the language goes unchallenged, the system will remain intact and the minds of American society will continue to be affected by the social conditioning of bigotry. The slaves had to learn to view all Anglo-Saxons (white), and European Americans as the people who controlled their lives as well as their deaths (not natural); that everything relative to them was considered normal; that they represented the normal human being and as such set the standards for life in American society. The things that gave the Anglo-Saxons, and European Americans the power and privileges aside from the laws they instituted, was their skin complexion and the language.

The language informed the African slaves that they were less than human beings; in fact, they were no higher than the animals. The language informed them that their black skin color was frightening, ugly, dirty, and smelly and more like that of the apes than humans. The language told them that their facial features were ugly and biologically not the same as the Anglo-Saxons' beauty. The African slaves were forced to accept or appear to accept these conditions whether they believed them or not.

Once physical slavery ended, the language, as well as the system of supremacy continued. As late as 150 years ago, an article appeared in the *Nation* magazine written by Taylor Lewis that made mention of the language and its continued effect of dehumanizing the African American: "Even when we advocate the cause of the African, we do it in a manner that would be though insulting and utterly undemocratic in any other case. We use the language of masters and owners." He added that "The way in which we speak to the colored man, and of the colored man, shows an unconscious yielding to the anti-Christian prejudice we are striving to overcome." So, the purpose and power of the language have never been a secret to many European Americans, but seemingly, remains to be one for many African American.

The system of European American, Anglo-Saxon (white) supremacy and African American inferiority continues to manifest its presence in the language. Real social progress will begin when we as a society learn to communicate with one another in an unbiased language.

Racism, The Gift That Keeps Supporting and Promoting Bigotry

July 31, 2018

One of the most common expressions heard today is the term racism. Without knowing or thinking about it, the use of that term does three things simultaneously, it underscores, promotes and supports the concept of European American (white) supremacy. Derived from the term race, racism, racist, and all the other terms associated with them serve as tools in the language to keep the concept of races alive and well. The use and acceptance of the word racism in American society underscore the false concept of the existence of multiple biological races, more specifically, it underscores the existence of a (black) African American and a (white) European American race, a concept that is totally without foundation and proof. The concept is an invention or social construction used to control society by conditioning the view of the European Americans as superior to African Americans and all people of color.

The term racism is and has always been inaccurate because it denotes something based on an illusion and myth. No such thing as multiple races exists, only the human race. The term racism refers to the psyche of a group, not an individual. So, anyone who identifies with a group that is represented as embracing that philosophy is referred to as racist. What occurs in the people who are identified as racist or who identify themselves as racist is based on three things: a sense of security, privilege, and power. The fact of the matter is that a racist is actually a selfish individualist who enjoys the comfort and protection of numbers as in his or her group, tribe, or organization for security and so feels free to exercise and enjoy the privileges and power afforded the group without fear of being accused of the bigotry represented in those privileges and power.

The numerous writers and scholars that develop theories and concepts relative to racism and racist thoughts and actions are simply supporting and promoting a Tooth Fairy myth. Since the concept of race is based on a myth and/or invention, all the research and writings about race contain a fallacy. The actions and behavior observed and studied, for certain, can be verified by some means, but those actions and behavior are not based on the group but the individuals who use the group mindset as a source of security. If we look at a number of so-called hate groups, we would find that they all have one thing in common, the concept of privilege and power based on skin color. Those privileges and power were and are derived from the abuse and exploitation of African Americans and other people of color. When hate groups finally discover that their life's objective is a fraud, that no such thing as a white race exists, they should come to understand the meaning of a fool's errand.

At one time in America, the term racism carried an undesired stigma and a sense of unacceptable behavior, since it was contrary to the precepts noted in the Declaration of Independence and The Constitution. However, what is also of concern is the fact that society embraced and practiced slavery and bigotry before, during and after the issuance of those documents. So, hypocrisy relative to the concepts of race and racism were conditioned in society as ordinary and acceptable. Once the bell of viewing people of color as less than human beings were rung, despite all the contrary actions like the 13th and 14th Amendments, and the various laws about civil rights, the reverberations of bigotry continue today.

Since the term racist is based on an unsubstantiated premise, it does not reflect the bias intended in its use. The appropriate terms are bigot and bigotry, not racist and racism. The use of the term racist relieves the person for which it is used relief from any personal responsibility. That relief comes from the fact that the individual represents his or her group's philosophy, not a personal or unique attitude. Therefore, any criticism of the individual racist is transferred to the group he or she represents. Because of the avoidance of direct responsibility, the term racist or racism enjoys the protection and security of the group. The same is not true of the terms bigot and bigotry because of the individuals labeled as such bear the direct responsibility for their thoughts, actions, and behavior.

The European Americans who identify themselves as racists also recognize that the privileges have been provided them through years of segregation, discrimination, and bigotry. The very first thing that comforts the racist is the fact that American society has been conditioned to reflect the social elements that support European American privileges from standards of beauty to behavior and comfort. Society has witnessed in recent times the reaction of some European Americans who felt discomfort in the presence of African Americans, so they had no reservation whatsoever is calling 911 and expecting to and having their concerns addressed. Whether they realize it or not, to exercise that kind of social control is called privilege.

The most important element at the racist's disposal comes from the group he or she represents, and that element is power. Through the efforts of groups, laws that favor their philosophy can be and have been made and passed as well as enforced. The efforts of many civil rights activists today are focused on changing many of the laws that were enacted to keep people of color in a state of inferiority. Fortunately, the powers of the racists and racism, in general, are beginning to feel the effects of a changing American society. The concept of race is finally beginning to deconstruct due to its mythical construction, the rapidly changing demographics, and the entrance into politics by people who want to see and live in a society that reflects the values this country promotes and represents—the rights of everyone to experience life, liberty, and justice.

We can all be an active part of the change that is taking place by realizing that the language we use helps to keep us ignorant and divided. Rather than using the word race, use ethnic group or ethnicity instead; in place of the words racism and racist, use bigotry and bigot. Small changes can make a big difference.

The Use of the Word Racism Precludes the Appropriate Use of the Word Bigotry

August 7, 2018

For far too many years we Americans have employed a term that did not reflect the actions and deeds of individuals represented by that term. The term is racism and as defined by most dictionaries resembles the following: "a belief that race is the primary determinant of human traits and capacities and those racial differences produce an inherent superiority of a particular race." In America race was described and identified by skin complexion of black and white with white deemed the superior of the two. Subsequently, whenever anything in society points to or indicates a privilege or advantage for the so-called white race (European American) over that of the so-called black race (African American) the act is labeled as an act of racism. If we were to follow the logic of the acts of racism, we might determine that the whole of the African/African American experience has been one of racism. All one needs to do to verify racism is to look at several significant legal adjustments made since the Civil War regarding the treatment of African Americans.

The term racism was taken from the term race which has been misappropriated and misinterpreted to justify its use relative to the superiority of the European Americans. The fact that the term is still in use today is owing to the social conditioning of American society that invented the social elements that underscored and guaranteed the essence of European American superiority. When we look at the history of social concerns such as jobs, education, housing, finance, to name a few, that were used to control the progress of the African Americans we realize that they were designed to keep the African American in a state of inferiority compared to the European American. For each of these social concerns African Americans had to fight in courts, usually, the Supreme Court, to finally receive some semblance of fairness. The fight was against the government, not individuals, and the fight was not against racism, but against injustice and bigotry.

African Americans and many conscientious Americans have been fighting since before the Civil War for justice and full citizen rights for African Americans and other people of color. Although the term racism has been employed as the cause of the bias, prejudice, and discrimination preventing full civil rights for African Americans the fact of the matter is that racism was just an excuse to maintain psychological control of the race concept and the perception of superiority. The reason for the persistence of the social concept of racism is because it is a belief, not an action or a thing. A belief cannot be destroyed; it must be replaced. An example of how a belief can remain unchallenged or in place is found in our view of the tomato, which for many years we thought to be a vegetable but in fact is a fruit. Nonetheless, in almost all supermarkets and grocery stores the tomato is placed in the vegetable produce section. By placing the tomato in the vegetable section, our false concept of it as a vegetable and not a fruit is reinforced. So, it is with the term racism that when we see it being employed we do not think about it reinforcing ethnic superiority, but simply focusing on some reference to social injustice.

Unlike the term racism that is based on a false concept, the term bigotry is free from any sense of illusion, myth or social invention. Bigotry is defined as a "stubborn and complete intolerance of any creed, belief, or opinion that differs from one's own." In other words, bigotry is the property of the individual, not a group and as such any act of bigotry reflects on the individual who owns total responsibility for the act or action. A bigot would possess the elements of narrow-mindedness, biases, and discrimination as part of that mindset. Here the difference between a bigot and a so-called racist is that while the racist only believes in ethnic superiority, the bigot acts on the biases to prove or underscore the belief.

The numerous incidents of European Americans calling 911 to report a person of color being in a place the caller thought was not appropriate for them to occupy demonstrates acts of bigotry. Any individual can possess a belief and never act on it, but once an act has been committed, the experience becomes real, not imaginary. Since racism is not a legitimate term relative to race by color, the appropriate term for the individual committing the biases act is a bigot and the belief system is bigotry.

To ethnically biased Americans the words racist and racism do not give a reason for pause because they serve as a compliment since it underscores their mindset. The social conditioning that many European Americans experience views ethnic bias and European American privilege as natural and right. When those concepts are challenged the European American automatically becomes defensive and strives to protect what is considered an infringement on their Constitutional rights. One can understand the European American's reaction because American society has spoon-fed the European American to view these privileges as ordinary, lawful, and socially acceptable. For example, when the Starbuck employee called 911 because two African American men in the store made her feel uncomfortable, her efforts were recognized and rewarded by the law enforcement officers when they arrived; they handcuffed the men and led them out of the establishment. Although the men were not charged and finally released, they had never done anything wrong in the first place, including not causing a disturbance. The employee who made the call was never made to view her feeling of discomfort as a part of her biased social conditioning.

When we look back at the definition of bigotry and bigot, we recognize that the bigotry of the Starbuck employee as well as most of the other incidents where European Americans that called 911 relative to the presence of people of color was what initiated the action against the people of color, not the belief that they belonged to a race superior. Bigots can be held responsible for their actions, racists not at all. In America, racism is a refuge for bigots.

The Power of Language Continues to Enslave American Society

August 21, 2018

One of the constant conundrums challenging America today is race; the reason for it being constant is because while we experience and observe it, we can only describe it, not defines it. We cannot define race because it is a concept based on conjecture and myths. Since the Greeks and Romans did not know why the sun rose and set every twenty-four hours, they made up a story about it. The story had some facts in it relative to the movement of the sun, but the facts were surrounded by fiction. Apparently, they thought that Apollo drove his chariot around the heavens riding up to the center of the sky in the morning, and down to the horizon at night. Fortunately, scientists came along to give more precise information about the sun and its relations to the earth. Today, the world knows the actual movement of the sun as well as the other celestial bodies in the universe and no longer need to invent myths. Unfortunately, we have not arrived at that point with the use of the term race. The myth continues because we have not decided to rid ourselves of its power to control our mind and bodies.

Language is the most important tool used in transmitting not only information but also a controlling influence over society. When the slave masters took away the slaves' identity, history, and culture, they forced on the slaves a language that was meant to keep them enslaved. The language was such an important tool that the slaves were forbidden to learn to read and write it. The punishment for anyone caught teaching a slave to read or write were heavy fines, whippings, or imprisonment, depending on the state in which it occurred. The slave owners knew that language as a tool could be used to control minds, but they also knew that it could also be used to liberate minds as well.

One way in which language was used to control society was when it constantly reminded European Americans that they were superior to all people of color, and it reminded people of color that they were inferior to European Americans. Once the captive Africans arrived in America and were stripped of their identities and past; they were forced to accept the reality of slavery. The language they used always pictured them as inferior and European Americans as powerful, privileged, and in total control of society. The African captives knew that they were not Negroes, blacks, or other terms associated with their identity, but they were defenseless to do anything about it for fear of repercussions, including death. After years of social conditioning in which the language constantly reminded the African Americans that they were Negroes, blacks, colored, and a host of other denigrating terms, their actual identity became less of a concern than their civil rights as citizens.

In the early 1960's language was used as a tool for protest by African Americans who combined identity with the fight for civil rights with the phrase "Black Power." Africans were forced to wear the identity of black from the beginning of American slavery and it was used as a derogatory and denigrating term. Even African Americans used the term as derogatory within the African American community. However, when the phrase "Black Power" was used by Stokely Carmichael during a 1960's civil rights rally, it gained legs and moved throughout the national African American community as well as society at large via music and media. The reference to "black" was used to engender a new sense of pride and positive value to what was once viewed as insulting and denigrating to African Americans. The power of language to influence worked to change the negative concept of blackness as an identity for African Americans to one of positivity, pride, and beauty.

While the language shift worked to provide a new sense of self for the African Americans relative to a black identity, it accomplished little for the European American since no change occurred in their conception and use of the word black as derogatory. The major misconception of the

African American community nationally was that the word black would somehow be transformed to represent a new identity. The problem with that happening is that the space the word black occupied in the language could and would not be replaced simply by repetition. Although European Americans could use the word white for their identity, it carried no negative connotations, just the opposite. Many Europeans abandoned their cultural identity to accept the white identity because of the power and prestige it provided them. African Americans because they did not use their cultural or ancestral identities were forced to be identified as blacks and Negroes. Two reasonable identity choices are African American or people of color, but only for ancestral identities. The cultural identity has always been American.

Many people of color in America accept the word black as a form of identity without realizing that the words black and white are adjectives, not nouns; that is, as nouns they represent colors, but as adjectives, they usually precede the noun race. Therefore, if the word black is used as a noun, it serves no purpose as an identity because it represents no cultural or ancestral ethnicity. If the word black is used as an adjective proceeding race, then the identity is based on a false concept of a black race that is viewed as a monolith which is also incorrect. In other words, the use of the slave masters' language still represents some control over society's identities.

The late Malcolm X learned that language as a social tool could provide an element of power and influence. So, he worked hard to become proficient in the use of language, and as a result was able to educate, enlighten, inform, irritate, and intimidate his audiences. Partly due to his early death he had not gained the level of understanding that would have helped to unlock the door of ignorance relative to how language managed to retain control of the concept of race. He did, however, recognized that the identity given the African captives upon their arrival was not their true identity and so he rejected his family name (usually taken from the slaves' former owner or master) and replaced it with the letter X which is symbolic for the unknown. American society's challenge now is to recognize how language has been used to control us, so we can set about the business of freeing ourselves. We cannot resolve a problem if we do not recognize that it exists.

Trump's Positive Contribution to a Better America Despite His Bigotry

July 25, 2018

One of the most important results of Donald Trump's election was America's recognition of its diverse population. For certain we all knew that America was a diverse population, but we were not as aware of the bigotry that existed within some Americans towards others. Trump did not create the bigotry, but he has been very instrumental in bringing it out in other people. Many Americans did not realize that they were bigots until Trump along with members of his administration and party began focusing on the concept of ethnic bigotry. Even today, many Americans do not realize or accept the fact that we have been socially conditioned to accept bigotry as normal as it pertains to people of color.

Regardless of the efforts of Trump to point out and comment on ethnic diversity in American society, because of the rapidly changing demographics, the fact would have eventually presented itself—America continues to change. The effect of America's changing demographics is like the bottom of a lake that has dried up because of a drought or being drained; a lot of debris is uncovered and what becomes visible for the first time in a long time speaks to a variety of discoveries. Many European Americans have never seen themselves as being biased towards other Americans for any reason. They might be considered ignorant since they lacked the knowledge of their social conditioning towards people of non-European heritage. That form of ignorance can be easily seen and experienced if these Americans live in a predominantly European American environment where they have little exposure to people of color or of diverse ethnicity. If nothing ever happens to call their attention to social and ethnic differences, then their perception will continue.

For many European Americans, ignorance is an excuse to continue to practice bigotry because they believe that they cannot be held responsible for something for which they are ignorant. Unlike the European Americans who are rarely exposed to ethnic differences, these European American are fully aware of the social privileges provided them because of their identity. However, when and if these European Americans are questioned about their display of social bias, they usually feign ignorance of their bias. Since they are not aware of their bias, they cannot be held responsible for their actions or judged negatively because of them; they believe that get a pass.

Another group of European Americans with biased social conditioning believe these biases to be normal and an accepted way of life. Rather than accept the social privileges they received as based on ethnic bigotry, they choose to ignore the reality and continue to accept the illusion of ethnic superiority as real. Anyone who challenges their view of society and the world is viewed as an enemy or at least suspect. We have over the past few years witnessed many instances of European Americans using their social privilege to call attention to their lack of comfort relative to an incident involving ethnic Americans of color. Unfortunately, many of their efforts are rewarded by the law enforcement establishment because they too, in many instances, share the same biases.

The biased social conditioning of many European Americans gives them a sense of not only privilege but also entitlement. Their sense of entitlement leads them to believe that they should feel safe and comfortable in all situations, and when they do not enjoy these feelings, they can call 911 and receive immediate satisfaction. To many of these Europeans Americans, they believe that they are not bigoted or biased; they are simply exercising their God-given rights as they interpret them. They have not accepted the fact that America is a diverse society and all Americans deserve the opportunity to exercise the same rights and privileges as they enjoy.

We Americans owe Trump and his administration a debt of gratitude for bringing out the problems relative to cultural biases that exist in society today. The warning America has been given relative to our diverse society is that we must learn to live together as brother and sisters or perish as fool unable to resolve our differences. What we must learn to accept is that all Americans are ethnic Americans and no one ethnicity is superior to another. The problems we face affect all Americans because they either add to or detract from us all regardless of our petty differences. Once the problems from the Trump experience are exposed, we will become aware of the challenges we must address to make certain we do not face the same ones again.

Ignorance is a key ingredient used by society to keep the status quo from succumbing to reality. For example, the contributions of African Americans to American society from Crispus Attucks to Katherine Johnson are quite relevant to our American story but mention either one to almost any educated European American and he or she would not recognize either name. Unfortunately, one could do the same with almost any educated African American with the same results. The problem is that knowledge of these individuals and their accomplishments would provide an element of pride in the African Americans and a sense of surprise in many European Americans. The fact that the information relative to these two Americans is available but not included in most American History books is due to both ignorance and bias. The ignorance represents a lack of knowledge; the bias represents a deliberate action to keep positive and image-influencing information from the readers.

American society, in general chooses, to ignore the factual information and knowledge relative to the myth of races but refuses to accept and promote it as an act of ignorance. Fortunately, facts and truth have a timely way of pushing ignorance to the side like water bursting from a dam overwhelms anything in its path. For American society, the changing demographics are like that dam water waiting to find its path. Ignorance can prevail for just so long before the truth comes in to replace it. When the truth comes, ignorance will be destroyed.

Why Steve Bannon Wants to be Called a Racist and Wear it as a Badge of Honor

March 17, 2018

For almost a decade this blog has advised readers to stop using the word racist because it was inaccurate and counterproductive. The fact is that when someone who has a bias against people of ethnicities different from his or her own is called a racist that serves to underscore, support, and compliment them and their beliefs. When people speak and behave in bias ways that show their bigotry towards other people, they can usually hide behind the word racist. Let us look briefly at what forms the basis of the word racist.

When the word race came into popular usage by the Anglo and Saxons with reference to the British, no concern for physical appearance was at issue. The word was used to signify a difference in character and social behavior. The British were referred to as "brutes" by the Anglo and Saxons with the understanding that their ancestries were totally different and not akin; that is, they did not want to be associated with them in any way. A change in the use and significance of the word race came into effect when slavery was introduced in Europe, and especially in England. As long as all people regardless of their skin complexion and social status were viewed as human beings' treatment of them showed respect for their humanity. Once, however, some people could be viewed as less than human, then, less humane treatment of them could be justified. So, the word race began to take on a different usage, one that took into consideration not only the character, and social status of people but also their skin color.

When the founding fathers introduced the concept of race by skin color, they did so base on nothing more than their desire to avoid having to justify slavery. The bias against people of low social and economic status was already in place before they left England. In order to have people of color viewed as inferior, the European American or Anglo-Saxons had to be seen as superior, hence, white supremacy. As long as European Americans controlled society, they could also control the concept of European American supremacy which they did through all the social institutions as well as through the churches. What the founding fathers did not realize was that their concept of race by skin color was flawed and based on simply a false concept that could not withstand the test of time, and their control would not last forever.

Consequently, today many European Americans conditioned by society to see themselves only through their skin color are being impolitely awakened to the reality of their delusion—no such thing as a black race and a white race exists. The only race of human in existence today, as far as we know, is human beings. Unfortunately, many European Americans who have for many years viewed themselves as superior to all people of color are unwilling to accept the fact that they were deceived about race. The deception has been such an integral part of American society that having to come to grips with reality is a monumental challenge.

For years, many groups in America have based their identity and social significance on the color of their skin and the concept of skin complexion being the basis of a biological race which they wish to preserve. The total number of groups are too numerous to name here, but a few that are generally known as white nationalist groups focus on white supremacist or white separatist ideologies, and they often focus on the alleged inferiority of people of color. A few of these groups include Ku Klux Klan, neo-Confederate, neo-Nazi, racist skinhead, Christian Identity, and Aryan nation among many more. These kinds of groups are not restricted to America but exist in parts of the world where the concept of a white race is cultivated. These groups are now experiencing pressure from the changing demographics around the world that debunk the concept of race. Their natural inclination is to fight back, which is what they are trying to do primarily through propaganda in a variety of forms.

In a recent article by Daniel Politi in The Slatest (3/10/2018) "Let Them Call You Racist…Wear it as a Badge of Honor," we learn that President Trump's "former chief strategist Steve Bannon told a gathering of the far-right in France that they should be proud of being called racists." Speaking to members of the French National Front party Bannon added: "Let them call you xenophobes. Let them call you nativists. Wear it as a badge of honor." Each of the labels focuses on the idea or concept of a mythical race of so-called white people. Bannon attempted to justify his advice to these far-right groups in general: "Why should members of the far-right wear the racist label as a badge of honor? 'Because every day, we get stronger and they get weaker,' Bannon told the crowd. In his travels throughout the world, Bannon has learned that 'history is on our side' because 'globalists have no answers to freedom.'" Bannon's philosophy defies rational and common sense in that he does not identify or define who the "other side "and the "globalists" are nor does he state the group's objective.

When Barak Obama became President of the United States, the fact that he was a man of color, an African American, sent a shock wave through the bigots of America and around the world. The shock was to their belief in European American/white superiority. While the myth of race and skin color representing symbols of superiority and inferiority have been debunked for many years, bigots have no rational way of accepting the reality that all human beings are brown; just different shades of brown. Hence, the foundation of their philosophy and belief in a white race and its superiority have no basis on which to sustain itself other than propaganda. With 80% of the observable world's population being people of color, and the rapidly changing demographics representing mixed ethnic populations, the numbers are greatly against Bannon and his like-minded followers.

Bannon and his followers enjoy being called racist because that word supports their philosophy of a white race; however, the use of that word also removes any direct responsibility of bias from the individual and assigns it to the so-called white race of which the individual is only a representative. The fact is that Bannon is not a racist, but a bigot, a word he does not use. He does not use it because it is accurate and places all responsibility for the bigotry on the individual, not a group, and it does not support a superiority concept. So, for the record, Bannon is not a racist, but a bigot.

———

What's Wrong with White People (European Americans)

October 27, 2017

Some European American people are in a quandary about what to do about their knowledge of bigotry and how it affects them. A few things to consider in attempting to address this conundrum involve an awareness of reality, and an awareness of language. To deal with reality is to understand that many European Americans do not realize that society has conditioned them to view themselves as the model of humanity or see themselves as not belonging to a race but as representative of humanity. That conditioning also has them view all people not like them as inferior to them. This conditioning is something that is acquired from living in a society that controls the social atmosphere and shows the European Americans how to see other people, what to think about other people, and how to behave around other people. Therefore, being biased against non-European people comes naturally and seems normal, nothing out of the unusual. For European Americans seeing themselves as the center of the universe is also normal. The awareness is that all the conditioning is base in falseness, myth, lies, illusion and it is bigoted.

They could not see the illusion because society presented everything to them as occurring naturally. The bigotry, segregation, discrimination and other abuses were present in society, but because they were viewed as normal to many European Americans, they did not feel compelled to do anything to address them as social and human wrongs. When the African Americans protested for civil rights, many of the European Americans remained silent although many of them were aware of the injustices African Americans were experiencing. Regarding civil rights legislation, not a single act or law was directed specifically to African Americans, but all Americans. Never the less, African Americans were implicated in every piece of civil rights legislation that included the word race; an action used to make certain the concept of races continued.

One of the ironies relative to bigotry in America involves the efforts of the civil rights organizations. While many European Americans did not support the protests of the civil rights activists, the major segment of society to reap the greatest benefits from the civil rights gains is the European American women as a result of Title IX of the 1964 Civil Rights Act. Today, some fifty years after the Civil Rights Act, African Americans experience the least success from Affirmative Action. For example, "The median white [European American] household has 13x as much wealth as the medium black [African American] household; and 10x as much as the medium Hispanic household. Even with a college education: The medium white [European American] person has 7.2x the wealth of a similarly educated black [African American] person." (The Nation, September 2017, p.5)

The challenge for many European Americans comes from finding ways to deconstruct the illusion they have lived under all their lives. Their initial response to this awareness might come as a shock, not wanting to believe that their lives have been a game of pretending. Shock is the appropriate term because the other stages of awareness follow the Kubler-Ross stages of grief. These stages are important because for European Americans coming to the awareness of their lives being an illusion and replacing that illusion with reality is similar to losing someone to death. The stages are shock, denial, anger, rejection, examination, understanding and acceptance.

Once the acceptance of reality has been achieved next comes how to deal with the reality. Language is the biggest threshold to overcome because we never questioned the language since we grew up with it. So, if European Americans called themselves white now, what will they call themselves instead of white? The ideal would be that they call themselves Americans. Here we must introduce the two identities we all have: a cultural and ancestral identity. The cultural identity is the one that we choose; the ancestral identity is based on the ethnicity of our birth parents. However, when the founding fathers invented the concept of race by color, both the cultural and ancestral identities was taken away and put in their place were the colors black and white. For many Europeans, the opportunity to call themselves white was worth giving up their identities; for African Americans, the choice was not available.

Unfortunately, many European Americans do not know that they have an ancestral and cultural identity; the only identity they know of is white. If that white identity is taken from them, they are left without a sense of value and worth. For those European Americans who know the value of white supremacy and white privilege, the fear of losing that white identity represents their reason for living. So, they become defensive when they believe that identity is threatened. Any social progress by African Americans and people of color represent to the bigots, a threat to their white privilege.

The constant challenge for America is that people of color see themselves as human beings, even when European Americans see only themselves as normal human beings; they see everyone else as different and abnormal. The problem is how they, the European Americans, see themselves and others, not how others see themselves and European Americans. European Americans have been socially conditioned to see people who do not look like them as inferior to them, and that conditioning, however, feels natural to them. Undoing the bigoted social conditioning of European Americans must be the responsibility of enlightened and knowable European Americans who know and understand the system of white supremacy. The primary starting point for undoing the social conditioning is with language, beginning with the words race, black and white. Once those words have been debunked, then the process of replacing the bigoted concept of white (European American) supremacy can begin.

In looking at the topic of this essay, how it is interpreted depends on what word or words are emphasized—wrong or white people (European American), and who is doing the interpreting.

The American System of Ethnic Injustice Slowly Being Revealed

June 11, 2015

Slices of reality are slowly being cut away from the apple of delusion that masquerades as American justice when we view the many videos showing how the law enforcement establishment denigrates the lives of African Americans. What we are witnessing via the videos is the system slowly being dismantled by its inability to maintain its creditability as a form of reality. The system was flawed when it was invented and put into motion by the founding fathers. For certain, the founding fathers knew that a lie could not last forever. Nevertheless, they believed that if they controlled society, there was little chance of the lie being discovered. What is the lie that characterized the system?

American society was created by people with biased attitudes towards people of color, but especially Africans with dark or black skin complexion. The historian Gary B. Nash noted in his book, *The Great Fear*, that the English were familiar with people of skin complexions darker than their own because of years of trading in the Middle East as well as North Africa. However, when the fair-skinned English encountered dark-skinned Africans, they reacted negatively:

Unhappily, blackness was already a means of conveying
some of the most ingrained values of English society. Black—and

its opposite, white —were emotion-laden words. Black meant foul, dirty, wicked, malignant, and disgraceful. And of course, it signified night—a time of fear and uncertainty. Black was a symbol signifying baseness, evil, and danger. Thus, expressions filtered into English usage associating black with the worst in human nature: the black sheep in the family, a black mark against one's name, a black day, a black look, to blackball or blackmail. White was all the opposites—chastity, virtue, beauty, and peace. Women were married in white to symbolize purity and virginity. Day was light just like night was black. The angels were white; the devil was black. Thus, Englishmen were conditioned to see ugliness and evil in black. In this sense their encounter with the black people of West Africa was prejudiced by the very symbols of color which had been woven into English language and culture over centuries (p 11).

The attitude described by Nash continues today to an appreciable extent because it was made part of the fabric of the European American psyche. Looking back through American history we learn that even though America made efforts to abolish slave trade in the 1770s, it was not until 1808 that Congress ended the trade. However, slavery did not end, and while slaves were controlled by their owners, the free African Americans were thought to represent problems. Nash noted that "After 1790 the free Negro, in both the North and the South, was subjected to increasing hostility, discrimination, and segregation. Once they had turned back abolitionist crusade of the revolutionary period white Americans became less concerned about the black slave than about black men who were not slaves." Nash underscored where that new concern led:

Southern states began passing laws prescribing heavier penalties for black felons than white, stripping away the legal rights of free Negroes, taxing free black men more heavily than whites, banning the free Negro from the polls and from political office, and forcing him out of white churches where he had been free to go and in some cases encouraged to go while a slave (p 25).

The European American had exerted total control over the African/ African American since slavery and the tool they used to justify that control was the invention of a white and black race. Any effort to free the African American would suggest that he was capable of living with European Americans on an equal basis; this proposition they would never concede because their entire belief system was based on black inferiority. Nash commented on the challenge to the European Americans' need for control once the African Americans were freed: "…they found themselves at the brink of giving up a system of control and a sense of mastery which they had come to believe was **natural and essential** to the well-being of their society." He continued: "It was almost as if the logic by which the African had been held in chains had been shattered. To compensate, a new system of control must be devised so that the free Negro, who remained a Negro after all, could be dominated almost completely" (p25). So, ethnic bigotry, race, was introduced into the American psyche as normal and correct.

America has always been perceived by European Americans as **their** country. All the other people who are not Anglo-Saxons are here through the Anglo-Saxons' generosity. Too often some Americans associate denigration of the African American with only the South, not so, said Ronald Takaki, author of "The Black, Child-Savage," he noted that the negative" image of the Negro served a need shared by whites, North and South; it performed an identity function for white Americans during a period when they were groping for self-definition." He continued:

> *It is significant to note the way that whites imagined the Negro in relation to themselves: the Negro was mentally inferior, naturally lazy, childlike, unwholesome, and given to vice. He was the antithesis of themselves and of what they valued: industriousness, intelligence, and moral restraint. These, of course, were values which whites associated with civilized society. (p 42)*

What do these references to history and some European American attitudes have to do with the previously mentioned videos. Simply this; that attitude is reflected in many of the actions of law enforcement today, regardless of the geographical location. So, we can recognize that behavior as part of a system. For over three hundred years officers have acted with impunity against African Americans. We also know that the law enforcement agents do not act independently, but under the auspices of an administration. The primary element that keeps this system operating is the false concept of races. Accepting the concept of races, invented by the founding fathers, ensures the continuation of ethnic conflicts. Fortunately, society is changing dramatically towards the devaluing of race.

The children and grandchildren of closet bigots were told the lie relative to democracy that life, liberty, freedom was for all people; that everyone should be respected and valued regardless who they were. So, now when these children and grandchildren see an injustice committed, they come to the aid of the victims, which is exactly what the bigots do not want to see. Many European Americans believe in a system of justice for all, not the one invented to control people of color. These European Americans did not learn that the system was to work only for them and that they are a part of it. So, now they want the American society they were told exist for all. The keepers of the system are fighting with everything they have to hold it in place, but it is too late; society continues to change. With every video recording an injustice against African Americans and other people of color, another slice of the apple is removed, and the reality slowly and painfully comes to the light.

The View Without

Part II

"We cannot solve our problems with the same
thinking we used when we created them."
~ Albert Einstein

Americans and the Challenge of the Criminal Justice System

November 13, 2017

When Americans think of the criminal justice system in America they usually recognize it as a reasonable, rational, and fair agency of society. What we often do not see relative to the criminal justice system is the American society that is represented by the criminal justice system. We focus generally on the law enforcement agencies or courts rather than the people in society that make-up and contribute to the system. The fact that most of the law enforcement agents, police, are set freed or shown as not guilty of killing unarmed African Americans reflect on the people responsible for adjudicating justice. We acknowledge that the culture of the criminal justice system in America is biased against African Americans, but the system reflects the biased society.

A case in point is that of Betty Jo Shelby, a European American (white) female and a former Tulsa police officer who was acquitted in the fatal shooting and killing of Terence Crutcher. According to media reports, Shelby was on duty when she saw an SUV that was stopped in the middle of the street, the vehicle belonged to Crutcher. We learn that "Shelby testified at trial that she was scared because Crutcher appeared to be under the influence of drugs, didn't obey her commands and looked like he was reaching inside his vehicle." (Justin Juoapavicus, Associated Press, 10/26/2017)

Videos of the incident did not coincide with Shelby's testimony in that Crutcher was shown to be at least fifteen feet in front of her with both of his hands up in the air; the windows of his SUV were rolled-up. A fellow officer was standing next to Shelby when she fired her weapon killing Crutcher. After Crutcher was shot, no aid or medical attention was given to check on his well-being until after several minutes had passed.

The fact that Shelby shot and killed Crutcher cannot be disputed since the incident was captured on video. However, the reasons for the shooting by Shelby can be brought into scrutiny relative to those adjudicating her case, the jury. For the court to acquit Shelby of the shooting leaves us to question their qualifications to make such a judgment. The primary reason for the shooting according to Shelby was her fear of Crutcher. How can we explain the jury's actions of a not guilty finding if police officers feel threatened or that their lives are in danger when an unarmed African American walking away from them with his hands in the air? If Shelby is simply afraid of African American men, then she should not be working in law enforcement or any other place where she will encounter African American men.

Since the jury accepted her defense of fear of African American men, we might assume that they consider it a legally accepted defense for European American (white) officers shooting people of color. What happens when officers walk into a supermarket or mall or church and there they see African American men? Do they fear for their lives in these circumstances as well and so would be justified in shooting them? Many of the videos in recent years have shown this to be the case. We must ask where is the reasoning, rationale, and justice for the actions of the jury?

One of the conclusions we must draw from these actions is that of ethnic bias of the jury. Since the majority of the jury make-up in American is European Americans (whites), we must also conclude that they do not represent for the African Americans a 'jury of their peers' but more a jury representing the European American (white) officers. Since fear of African Americans and people of color appears to be a problem for many European American (white) law enforcers, why are they hired? And if hired, why are they not educated to treat people of color with the same decency and respect they would give other citizens?

The answer is simply because of their social conditioning which underscores the privilege accorded to them, European Americans (white), for their skin complexion. Simultaneously, European Americans (whites) are conditioned to view people of color as inferior in general, but to view African Americans with fear, anger, and dream because they are dangerous. Many European Americans (whites) do not realize their bigotry because their acquisition was acquired through everyday life at home, school, church etc. As a cognitive scientist, Justin L. Barrett, noted, "What we learn through testimony or through behavioral imitation is importantly influenced by social context biases." He added that "we model our thought and behaviors on others based upon what we perceive most others think and do (conformity bias), favor prestigious individuals for role models (prestige bias) and prefer to ape those whom we see as similar to ourselves or whom we want to be (similarity bias)." So, to many European Americans (whites) ethnic bigotry is not something that is unusual or viewed as out of the ordinary life experience.

What we find puzzling about the actions of the Americans citizens who serve as part of the criminal justice system is how they equate reason, rationale, and justice with their actions. For example, shortly after being acquitted for the shooting and killing of Terence Crutcher, that portion of Betty Shelby's record will be removed, and subsequently, will be expunged: "District Judge William LaFortune also ordered all documents involving former Tulsa officer Betty Jo Shelby's case sealed and kept with the court. The case will only be accessible through a court order and can be destroyed after 10 years, according to the law." (Justin Juoapavicus)

What we can observe from Shelby's case is that after shooting and killing an innocent American citizen because she was in fear, not threatened or felt to be in harm's way, she was acquitted of all charges and walked away from the incident with no repercussions. We have learned that she has been recently employed in a law enforcement position in a nearby town. In 10 years, no one will even know what she did except the family and friends of Terence Crutcher, Shelby, and the jury. After all, it was incumbent on the jury to administer a finding based on reason, rationale, and justice, but they failed in every respect. We, Americans, cannot allow this form of injustice to continue because whether we realize it or not, the mistreatment of any American affects us all. Act–find a way to make a difference.

The Problem with an Assumed Colorblind Society and Social Justice

November 4, 2016

For years now, this blog has been trying to make clear the misconception and lack of understanding relative to why any effort to fight racism is wasted time and energy. The reason racism cannot be fought or manipulated is because it is not a thing, but a concept. The founding fathers invented and instituted the concept of race by identifying two races, one white and the other black. The reasons for the concept of race were to maintain the power and control of American society. That power and control were represented in a system known as white supremacy with whites being the normal and natural human beings, superior to all non-white people, and blacks being inferior to all people, especially whites. As instituted, it was a system of ethnic bigotry constructed to promote and protect itself. One of the primary features of this system was the belief in the naturalness and normalcy of the supremacy by whites. The question regarding the validity of the term race and races as used by the founding fathers was seldom raised. So, everyone assumed that the term race used as social identity was legitimate and based in fact. So, many Americans never realize that their conception and perception of reality was false and biased towards people of color.

When the subject of racism or white supremacy is brought to public scrutiny, it is often described as being a fabric of American society. An example of how the system of bigotry works can be seen in the words and works of Chief Justice of the Supreme Court, John Roberts Jr. In an article by Stephanie Mencimer, "Colorblind Justice," (Nov/Dec 2016 Mother Jones) we learn how Justice Brown's conception of race influences his work. She noted Robert's effort in "gutting a civil right law he has been fighting his entire career." She continues her claim by stating that "Roberts has argued that the United States has become colorblind to the point where aggressive federal intervention on behalf of voters of color is no longer necessary—and this case, *Shelby County v. Holder,* was the pinnacle of that crusade." One wonders how a society that has and still uses the terms black race and white race as social identities can be considered a colorblind society.

The invention of races by color is the glue that continues to challenge the well-being of American democracy by preventing society from moving forward without regard to skin color. The concept of whiteness and blackness forms the core of many European Americans identities. So, how can America be colorblind? What justice Roberts does not realize is the fact that he has viewed America through biased eyes for all his life as something normal. In essence, because he is biased and does not realize it, his words show a lack of understanding of reality. Perhaps a little more information about Roberts' background will help us to better understand his words and actions.

Mencimer noted that "Roberts honed his views on race and voting as a clerk for Justice William Rehnquist, a man who as a court clerk himself had written a memo endorsing *Plessey v. Ferguson,* the 'separate but equal' doctrine upholding segregated schools." So, for Roberts, the concept of separate races was valid and correct for American society. Because of his views in opposition to civil rights laws, Rehnquist used his "commitment to color-blindness, and he used this theory to undermine the 1965 Voting Rights Act." Roberts shared this view with Rehnquist. The problem with Roberts' shared views with Rehnquist is the contradiction of identifying people as black and white and then saying that we live in a colorblind society where skin color does not matter.

To underscore the point of this blog in pointing out the lack of awareness of a biased perception by many Americans, including Justice Roberts we reference his actions relative to voting rights: "Echoing Rehnquist, Roberts has long insisted the United States has achieved a postracial, colorblind society, a point he emphasized in his 2013 majority opinion in *Shelby County v. Holder.* For Roberts to refer to America as a postracial society is to admit that prior to becoming a postracial society, it was a racial one. What evidence does he provide to mark or note society's transition from racial to postracial or from color to color blindness? None whatsoever. Roberts does not recognize or understand the system of European American (white) supremacy and African American (black) inferiority of which he is and has been a part of for all his life.

One way to try to understand the delusion and hypocrisy relative to race in America is the see how the system of supremacy was invented and how it continues today. Picture a tree with its parts represents American society: roots, trunk, branches, and leaves. The roots of the tree represent race; the trunk of the tree racism, the branches of the tree represent all the area of American society: government, education, science, education, law etc. Looking at that picture of the tree and its parts, what becomes apparent is the fact that the false concept of race has been the root of America's problem since the beginning. Therefore, trying to fight racism is impossible in America without recognizing that the tree is not and has never been real, just assumed so. As Americans, we have been socially conditioned to see that tree as real, but to ignore the fact that the term race is not valid or factual relative to mankind and skin color. For America to overcome its problem of ethnic bias, the false tree must be replaced with a tree that reflects the reality that does not begin by identifying people of color as inferior or of a different race.

Justice Roberts' view of America retains and promotes the system of ethnic bigotry because he refuses to recognize its existence. Roberts 'actions and words regarding voting right laws, for example, indicates that he is not blind to color, but justice. He does not see the whole picture of the American experience. "He probably still believes he is right, because he likely sees what is going on as simple partisan politics," says Hasen (Richard Hassen, a University of California-Irvine law professor who specializes in election law). "But for many of us, we see a world in which it is once again getting harder, not easier, for people—especially people of color—to cast a ballot which will count." How's that for a colorblind society and social justice.

Georgia Cop's Statement "We Only Shoot Blacks," Underscores Culture Bigotry

September 17, 2017

Many European Americans are beginning to see and realize the attitude and treatment received by African Americans from law enforcement. For too many years African Americans have been made to look like the evil and dangerous villains that deserve the abuse and even death they receive from law enforcement. When African Americans complained about the injustice and bigotry of the criminal justice system, many European Americans turned a blind eye and deaf ear to those complaints. Today, with the benefit of video technology the public can witness the behavior of law enforcement agents and their treatment of people of color. A recent incident involving a police officer and an assumed European American woman provides evidence to support the problem of ethnic bigotry in America.

An article by Terence Cullen in the *New York Daily News* (8/31/2017) told about the incident that underscores many of the claims against law enforcement and the deaths of many African Americans. The officer involved in the incident was Cobb County (Georgia) Lt. Greg Abbott and the article noted that "Abbott pulled the sedan over on suspicion of driving under the influence and told a woman in the passenger seat to use the cell phone in her lap. The woman tells the 28-year veteran she's afraid to move her hands. 'I've just seen way too many videos of cop,' the woman says before Abbott cuts her off. 'But you're not black' he says. 'Remember, we only shoot black people." The officer's comments tell us much about him and our society.

One of the first things the officer does with respect to his comment about the woman not being black is to show his biased social conditioning relative to the concept of races. He does not question the authenticity of the concept; he simply accepts it and proceeds with his beliefs. All Americans have been conditioned to accept the concept of races, black and white, as legitimate when we know that the concept is false, an invention to control society. By the officer identifying the woman as white, he has made a judgment about her that gives her power and privilege over people of color whether she wants it or not. The only reasonable assumption we can make about this officer's comment relative to the woman not being black is to consider her skin complexion. We can safely assume that her complexion is deemed by the officer acceptable enough to be considered white. Whether the woman is European American or a member of some other ethnic group, we do not know. However, that determination is of little consequence to the officer who has already made his judgment relative to her identity.

American society has conditioned European Americans to view African Americans as inferior to them. As such, the need to show respect and curtsey to them is never an issue because no repercussions result from disrespecting and abusing them. This attitude of bigotry is not something taught to each generation but shown in our way of life as being natural and normal. We ignore the facts that we are one race of people, facts given to us through the sciences, history, and even the Bible. Because the people who invented this system of bigotry also controlled all the institutions in society, they were able to keep the system alive and well. Today, many European Americans would not know their identity if they were told that they were not white; that is how extensive the social conditioning has become. They also believe that regardless of the educational, economic and political status people of color attain, the European Americans with no comparable credits is made to believe they are better. So, the color white is important to the officer as well as to the woman in the car.

Community relations have never been good between the African American community and the law enforcement community because law enforcement has always viewed African Americans as inferior. When one side of a community has preconceived ideas about the other that places them at a disadvantage, no reasonable or mutually just solution to any problem will be forth –coming. Most community relation programs instituted by law enforcement for the African American community always favor law enforcement because of their conditioned biases. Although some members of law enforcement desire to faithfully perform their jobs, they cannot deny that the culture inside of law enforcement is anti-black (African American) and that sentiment is reflected in the officer's statement: "Remember, we only shoot black people."

Norm Stamper, a retired European American police officer, noted in his book, *Breaking Rank*, (2005) that contrary to what European Americans believe, "Simply put, white cops are afraid of black men. We don't talk about it, we pretend it doesn't exist, we claim 'color blindness,' we say white officers treat black men the same way they treat white men. But that's a lie." Stamper's comments are underscored by another former member of law enforcement. In his book, *Choke Hold*, (2017) Paul Butler, an African American former federal prosecutor and law professor at Georgetown University, defined chokehold as laws and social practices made to control African American men: "It is a two-step process. Part one is the social and legal construction of every black man as a criminal or potential criminal. Part two is the legal and policy response to contain the threat—to put down African American men literally and figuratively." Given their experiences in law enforcement, these two individuals have no reason to make false statements about the culture of law enforcement regarding African Americans.

Officer Abbott, a 28-year veteran on the Police force, exhibited the ethnic bias that is part of the culture in which he works. Since he was conditioned by society to be biased against people of color, joining the police force did nothing to relieve him of his biases but, evidently, provided an environment in which they could be exercised with impunity. Removing Abbott from the force will not eliminate the problem of bigotry since it is societal. Whether we interpret Abbott's statements as sarcastic or not, they flowed freely from his mouth without hesitation. Abbott does not simply represent law enforcement, he represents American society. Until American society can label this biased culture despicable and stand together demanding justice for all our citizens, we must share in the responsibility of what this culture produces.

Police Unions Try to Control Department Culture Which Can Create Problems

September 7, 2016

The time has come for Americans to look at the arrogance, ignorance, and bigotry exhibited by members of the law enforcement establishment, in particular, the police union representatives. Santa Clara Police union and Police Chief differ on their responsibility: "The Santa Clara police chief has vowed to continue providing a safe environment at San Francisco home games after the union representing his officers threatened to boycott policing the stadium if the San Francisco 49ers don't discipline Colin Kaepernick for criticizing police and refusing to stand during the national anthem." (AP 9-4-2016) The union took the first action relative to Kaepernick's protest by sending a letter to the 49ers.

The police chief understands and accepts Kaepernick's Constitutional right to protest: "As distasteful as his actions are, these actions are protected by the Constitution. Police officers are here to protect the rights of every person, even if we disagree with their actions." On the other hand, the union representatives letter requested that action is taken against Kaepernick or else "it could result in police officers choosing not to work at your facilities." The union does not work for the city, the chief does.

If we were to go back and examine each of the cases of African Americans being killed or treated unjustly by law enforcement agents in cities like Ferguson, New York, Baltimore, Detroit, Los Angeles, etc...., we would also find a representative of their union stepping into the situation and doing several irrational things in favor of their officers. First, the union wants to separate the victims from the officers by underscoring the dangers involved in police work and the obvious disregard for the law by the victims. A picture of the police officers is painted of them being above the law and not worthy of criticism by the victims or the public; they are held as sacrosanct.

Once this picture of the police officers is presented, the union then attempts to turn the victim into the villain by checking to see if he or she has a police record that can be used to vilify him or her to the public. Although any information on a victim's record might not be pertinent to the incident in question, if it will cast a negative image of the victim, it will be used. The objective is to question the worthiness of the victim or the public to challenge the character of the police and turn the process of the public having to choose the "good guys," police, over the "bad guys," the victims. In any event, any aspersions cast upon the police officers are taken as criticism against the entire law enforcement establishment with no middle ground. The union knows that in the past, most people believed the police over the victim.

With Kaepernick's protest, the union had already decided that he was wrong and a villain to the point that if nothing was done by the 49ers organization to punish him, his entire team would suffer as well as all the people associated with their home games. The union totally disregarded Kaepernick's Constitutional right to protest in the manner he chose and because they did not approve of it, it was unacceptable. Fortunately, the police chief used better judgment and knowledge of the law to handle the situation. The chief's letter probably did not sit well with the union because it took away the union's power to instill fear in and to coerce victims of police misdeeds.

At times it seems that the union representative wants to take charge of any negative situation involving police officers and usurp the powers of the chief. For example, in Oklahoma City, the question of how police body cameras are to be used has caused some disagreement between the union representative and the chief. The union wants the police to have total control of the pictures recorded by these cameras—what is seen and by whom. The chief disagrees with that notion because the public would argue the benefits of the cameras if the pictures could be censured by the officer before, during and after a police action. The concept of transparency would be lost if the pictures could be altered before anyone other than the police could see them. No decision has been made in this case and because no decision has been made, the cameras are not being worn.

Often what the union representative does is to try and convince the public to believe the opposite of what he accuses a victim of during—painting everyone with one brush. For example, when a person accuses an officer of wrong-doing, the emphasis is on that officer, but the union tries to spin the story to make it appear that the entire police department or all law enforcement agencies are being indicted. Using this tactic, the union can create an "us" versus "them" scenario with "us" being the good guys, and "them" being the crooks. A quick reference to the union's letter to the 49ers underscores that point. According to the AP article, "the police union complained that Kaepernick's 'inappropriate behavior' has 'threatened our harmonious working relationship.'" The letter seeks to make Kaepernick the outsider –crook and the police the good guys. Fortunately, the police chief did not allow his power to be usurped by the union this time.

In his book, *Breaking Rank*, Norm Stamper commented on police unions as I noted in my book: "Police unions represent a problem for social change in America because they have been able to manipulate the system of [European American] white supremacy…they usually oppose any changes in their operation not introduced by themselves and complain when any criticism is directed toward them.…If any questions are raised concerning the actions of officers, the union usually accuse the party asking the question of being anti-police." According to Stamper, the unions usually try to control the culture of the police departments (*The System of European American (white) Supremacy and African American (black) Inferiority*).

The fact that the Santa Clara Police Union decided that Kaepernick's behavior was inappropriate and that some corrective action had to be taken shows the arrogance of the union. They used their position and standing in the community to make a value judgment against someone who had done no wrong. They showed their ignorance in sending a letter to the 49ers making a threat for some corrective action against Kaepernick before they checked to see if a law was broken or an offense committed. Although the question of Kaepernick's ethnicity was not mentioned, his protest involved the treatment of African Americans and people of color by law enforcement. The union took offense to his protest.

Reasons Why European American (White) Police Shoot and Kill African Americans

March 31, 2018

The police officers shooting and killing an unarmed African American man in Sacramento, California recently should come as no surprise to anyone who has been following the news the last four to five years. The excuses for the shootings are always the same: the officers reveal that they feared for their lives or they felt their lives were threatened, or the victim made a threatening gesture or movement towards them or they thought he or she had a gun in their hands. All of these reasons are viewed as justifiable for the shooting of a suspect. On the other hand, the family of the victim always asks the questions: why did you not wait to assess the situation before you fired shots? Why did you not use another of the tools available to you like the tazer, rubber bullets, nightstick, and bean bags? Why could you not have shot him or her in the arm or leg or some non-deadly place? Why did you not give the victim time to respond to your commands?

The fact that this scenario keeps happening repeatedly is not an accident or the action of a few bad officers but part of a culture that permeates the entire criminal justice system. Most officers know that regardless of their actions, their department and union will always take their word as valid over any citizen, so the fear of serious repercussions for a wrong deed does not represent an impediment to their actions. The American public has witnessed many times the results of a police shooting via video that contradicts the report of the officers. Yet, the officers walk away without being held responsible for the misdeeds committed. To blame be officers for not being held responsible for their deeds is not their fault but the system that supports them including the Attorney General, District attorney, prosecutor, judge, jury, and society.

What many African Americans understand about the criminal justice system in American is that it has always been biased against them as clearly recorded by history from before Reconstruction, the Black Codes, and Jim Crow. Many European Americans generally support law enforcement actions without question and by doing so allow injustices to continue against people of color. Some present and former police officers have readily admitted that a culture of hate, fear, anger, and bigotry against African Americans exist in law enforcement. From where do these feelings derive? The most obvious answer identifies social conditioning as the primary contributor to ethnic bias in American society that is retained by people who become part of the criminal justice system directly and indirectly.

Norm Stamper, a former police officer and author of the book *Breaking Rank* (2005) underscored the European American law officers' perception of the African Americans: "Simply put, white cops are afraid of black men. We don't talk about it, we pretend it doesn't exist, we claim 'colorblindness,' we say white officers treat black men the same way they treat white men. But that's a lie. "These feelings are not reserved for European American law enforcers only. Paul Butler, in his book *Choke Hold* (2017), noted that recent scientific research shed some light on how many African Americans are generally perceived: "When people see black men they don't know, they have a physical response that is different from their response to other people. Their blood pressure goes up and they sweat more. When a white person sees an unfamiliar black male face, the amygdala, the part of the brain that processes fear, activates." Earlier studies also indicated that the negative reactions of European American law officers towards African American males may because by unconscious social bias rather than deliberate actions.

Michelle Alexander in her book *The New Jim Crow (2013)* noted that several studies showed how some European Americans reacted to images of European Americans and African Americans in an exercise that considered observation, interpretation, and reaction. She noted, "that racial schemas operated not only as part of conscious, rational deliberations, but also automatically—without awareness or intent." This study might possibly explain why some European American police officers act irrationally when having to deal with African Americans and people of color in general:

One study, for example, involved a video game that placed photographs of white and black individuals holding either a gun or other object (such as a wallet, soda can or cell phone into various photographic backgrounds. Participants were told to decide as quickly as possible whether to shoot the target. Consistent with earlier studies, participants were more likely to mistake a black target as armed when he was not, and mistake a white target as unarmed, when in fact he was armed. This pattern of discrimination reflected automatic, unconscious thought processes, not careful deliberations (p. 107)

The fact that ethnic bias is central to the social conditioning in America accounts for the unconscious bias of many European Americans; that bias can be manifested either implicitly, explicitly or both. Consequently, many European Americans can honestly believe that they are not biased against African Americans because many of their friends, relatives, and associates are African American, however, that fact does not mean they are free of biases. Alexander noted that "Implicit bias test may still show that you [European Americans] hold negative attitudes and stereotypes about blacks, even though you do not believe you do and do not want to. In the study described above, for example, black participants showed an amount of 'shooter bias' like that shown by whites" (107). Of course, fewer European Americans are shot and killed by African American police officers than by European American officers.

Armed with the scientific information from the various studies mentioned, we can assert that much more than police training is necessary to replace the biased ethnic culture in our criminal justice system. The problem of ethnic bias must be the first item on the agenda to be addressed, not through training, but education. Society must fully understand and reject the bias before it can begin to replace it.

Trump's Statement to Police Underscores Ethnic Bias in Criminal Justice System

August 6, 2017

What are Americans to think when their President tells law enforcement members to break the law and abuse citizens who have been arrested and when questioned about his statements, they are passed off as if they were jokes? Why would the President want to joke about asking or telling the police to break the laws they are hired to enforce and follow and to abuse the citizens while doing so? To make matters worse, the President aimed his words for the unjust, unlawful, and abusive treatment of people of color. Through his comments, he gave permission to police officers to express their ethnic biases with physical violence and abuse of the people of color.

European Americans have been conditioned to view African Americans as criminals and less than first-class human beings. The media since before the Civil War have pictured and described African American in a negative and unflattering context. That practice still exists today, to a great extent. So, when the President made the statement about police officers throwing thugs in the back of a "Paddy wagon" (his words which are considered a pejorative phrase regarding the Irish) the immediate reference goes to Freddie Gray, the young African American man who died from injuries incurred from being put in a police van without proper restraints. None of the police officers were held responsible for Gray's death. So, the President, evidently, saw nothing wrong with the way citizens, especially African American citizens, are treated by the police.

A point of interest relative to the President's statement is the fact that he used the term "those thugs" rather than citizen or person. The term "thug" when used in a certain context and by certain people like the President, is a direct reference to African Americans. In his recently released book, ***CHOKEHOLD* [Policing Black Men]** Paul Butler, a former prosecutor and presently a Georgetown University Professor, devoted a chapter of his book on "Constructing the Thug." In that chapter, he explained that "the construction of the thug [is] based on the presumption that every African American man is a criminal. It is important to remember that this is a rebuttable presumption: African American men can do things to communicate that we are not dangerous." In addition, he added that "It would not be an understatement to say that the clear majority of black men engage in those kinds of performances every time we step out of the house. It's also true that many people can and do treat individual African American men with respect and kindness." The overwhelming sentiment relative to police behavior towards African Americans is based on fear, anxiety, and the presumption of them as criminals. Those feelings are enough to clear the bar and justify the unjust, unlawful, violent, and abusive treatment of African Americans.

When the President made his statements relative to how the police officer should treat 'thug's he was standing in front of a large number of police officers. To the surprise of many top law enforcement agents, police chiefs, and others in authority, many of the officers in the President's background smiled and applauded their approval of his comments. Why? Many applauded because they felt relieved that the President agreed with the way some police officers treat African American citizens. The comments served as encouragement to officers to continue their unlawful and abusive treatment of citizens of color. One wonders if some of those officers joined the force, not to protect and serve, but to harass and punish African Americans for being African Americans.

Many of the police chiefs and enforcement leaders were quick to call the Presidents statements, not in keeping with the law and practices of law enforcement and issued statements to the effect that their departments will not tolerate the rough treatment of prisoners nor will violations be taken lightly. Other police leaders underscored the fact that training focused on treating all citizens with respect and dignity.

Not all police officials felt the President's statements were out of order: "For example, Detective Stephen Loomis, president of the Cleveland Police Patrolmen's Association, excused Trump's comments in a statement to CNN as 'completely taken out of context by the racially exclusive and divisive profiteers' seeking to question Trump's support of all law-abiding citizens..." Loomis included "the law enforcement officers that live and work among [law abiding citizens] them." In other words, as far as Loomis is concerned all law enforcement officers are perfect; they make no mistakes or break laws and arrest only citizens who break the law. Everyone, according to Loomis, should realize that the President was simply joking when he made those comments. The concept of innocent before proven guilty for those arrested seems to have lost its value among some police union representatives.

The President's comments, whether serious or not, makes the assumption that when police officers arrest African Americans and people of color that official protocol can be dispensed with in favor of officers acting as judge, jury, and executioner. In many of the recent video showing police abuse of African Americans and other people of color, male and female, law-abiding citizens see for themselves how some citizens of color are treated by some law enforcement officers. If the trend continues, one will have to ask where the law-abiding officers are hiding. Many American citizens turn a blind eye and a deaf ear to these unlawful and abusive happenings simply because they think they are not directly implicated in them. However, nothing could be further from the truth because when an officer is caught breaking the law and he or she is exonerated from a criminal quilt, many are sued and found guilty in civil court. The involvement of the law-abiding citizen comes into play when an officer and his or her department are sued in civil court.

The cost to the uninvolved law-abiding citizens for not holding the criminal justice system responsible for the abuses committed by its officers is large and growing. Unfortunately, many African Americans and other people of color have suffered abuse and often death at the hands of police officers and in return sued the police in civil court. Recently, in Oklahoma City, two African American men who had their murder convictions overturned have both sued the state for $32 million each. One former inmate has already settled his case; the other is yet to be adjudicated.

When the unlawful, unjust, and abusive treatment of citizens start to make a greater impact on the uninvolved law-abiding citizens, then they will join with citizens working to change the criminal justice system and make it serve all citizens fairly, justly, and lawfully. Living in a democracy requires all to learn that injustice for some is an injustice for all.

No Justice from 'A Jury of One's Peers' in U. S. Court System

July 14, 2017

Recently in Tulsa, Oklahoma, a judge declared a mistrial, for the third time, in a case involving a European American former police office, Shannon Kepler. The officer acknowledged shooting Jeremey Lake, a 19-year-old African American male who had been dating Kepler's daughter, Lisa. While Kepler claimed that he was defending himself when he shot Lake, no weapon was found on Lake or anywhere near the scene. An article on abcnews.go.com provided the following information: "Kepler, who retired from the force after he was charged, was a 24-year-police veteran who said he was trying to protect his daughter, who had run away from home and was living in a crime-ridden neighborhood."

Americans in general and African Americans in particular, should not be surprised at the mistrial or even a not guilty decision from this trail and the many others involving African American men and police officers. We should realize by now that the criminal justice system, especially the courts were not meant to serve justice to people of color. We must be constantly reminded of the fact that American is a biased society and that people of color are viewed as objects that cause fear and anxiety to European Americans. Many of our laws, regardless of what they might intend, are meant to keep the concept of two different groups of people separated.

That separation is underscored in the court system and especially the jury system in America.

For African Americans as well most Americans in general, the phrase "A jury of one's peers," is meaningless, and because it is meaningless, few people ever experience having a member of his or their jury a peer. In an article by Eric Peters (3/23/2012), "A Jury of One's Peers," he notes that while this phrase is not found in our Constitution, the concept comes from English Common Law from which our Constitution was based. The phrase was intended to describe a situation where "The men of a community would gather to weigh evidence presented against someone—someone they knew. Unfortunately, what we have today is an altogether different animal. You may find yourself tried in front of a jury—but they will not be your peers."

Today, in Oklahoma, anyone 18-years-old and older with a valid driver's license can be randomly selected to serve on a jury. The individuals are not selected from a particular community, but usually from the county in which they live. If members of a jury were selected from specific communities where people of similar social, religious, economic, political, and education tend to live, then individuals facing charges from those communities would have a reasonable chance of being judged by a peer. Unfortunately, that is not the way things work.

In America, three things work against African Americans when they involve European American police officers, and juries—a lack of people of color on the jury, law enforcement bigotry, and systemic cultural bigotry. Most juries will consist of few people of color for any number of reasons, first of which is availability. Fewer people of color are chosen (at random) for jury duty and few are chosen to serve on a jury once reporting for jury duty. The lack of representation of people of color on the jury for an African American can make a difference in the jury's final decision. Also, the presence of one or two persons of color serving on a jury of predominately European Americans can be intimidating and stressful to them.

In his recently published book (2017), **CHOKEHOLD,** Paul Butler, a former prosecutor and law professor at Georgetown University, stated that "Cops routinely hurt and humiliate black people because that is what they are paid to do. Virtually every objective investigation of a U.S. law enforcement agency finds that the police, **as policy,** treat African Americans with contempt." He further stated that "The most problematic practices of American criminal justice—excessive force by police, harsh sentencing, the erosion of civil liberties, widespread government surveillance, and mass incarceration—are best understood as measures originally intended for African American men." The many jury verdicts involving the shooting by law enforcement agents have demonstrated that the repercussions for a European American or an officer killing a person of color are little and none, which underscores Butler's point. The fact that European American law enforcement agents use the aspect of fear in their defense of their actions is one that does not differ from the fear that European Americans experience generally when coming into contact with an African American male.

European Americans are socially conditioned to view African Americans with fear and dismay unless the African Americans are known to the European Americans. This conditioning is a natural and a normal part of everyday life and not viewed as a bias towards people of color. Butler referenced in his book a study entitled "Transforming Perceptions: Black Men and Boys," by the American Values Institute (3/2013), that noted the following: "When people [European Americans] see black men they don't know, they have a physical response that is different from their response to other people. Their blood pressure goes up and they sweat more." He also noted another study that stated: "When a white person sees an unfamiliar black male face, the amygdala, the part of the brain that processes fear, activates." So, the reference to the fear experienced by European Americans law enforcement as noted is part of the American experience for them and bad news for African Americans. The challenge for all Americans is to replace that fear with reason and understanding, knowing that we all belong to the same family of mankind. We must all work to replace the present criminal justice system or continue to be victims of it.

Consequently, we need to practice justice and respect towards one another because we realize as Peters noted: "Court proceedings should, of course, be impartial—but not to the extent of being obtuse. And obtuse -even evil—is precisely what we have today. Mindless worship of statutes as opposed to the spirit animating them. No harm done (or intended) no longer matters. Just 'the law'—as interpreted by twelve random strangers." While we can no longer practice the concept of "a jury of one's peers," we can certainly underscore the humanity we all possess. We must be the change we need.

Terrence Crutcher and the Tulsa Jury, Another Instance of Injustice by Reason of Being African American

May 19, 2018

The jury in Tulsa found Betty Shelby not guilty and in doing so told the world that African Americans and other people of color have no rights that a police officer need to respect. Once an African American is stopped by a police officer, his or her life is forfeited to that officer. Facts and evidence play no part in the reason for killing an African American by a police officer if we follow the accounts of the shooting of Terrence Crutcher.

Once police officers stop African Americans, the African Americans lose the right to speak because anything they say can be interpreted by the officers as disrespectful or threatening, whichever they choose. The African Americans lose the right to move because any movement might be seen as a threat to the officer's life. So, what can the African Americans do when stopped by a police officer? A frequently used bit of advice is to comply with the officer's command. The problem with that is if the African American starts the compliance too slowly then the officer is forced to act. That action might involve the use of a taser. When someone is shot with a taser, he must remain perfectly still, or his movement will be seen as resisting arrest and not complying with the officer's command. In other words, the African Americans are damned by whatever they say or do as far as the police are concerned.

Some people will say that no one loses his or her rights when stopped by a police officer. If that is not the case, then why are the victims of a fatal police shooting always viewed as guilty of a crime when they never had an opportunity to present their side of the event that led to the shooting? The victim's side is always challenged even with clear and concise video shows what happened. The problem is with the justice system and the non-thinking jury that fails to use common sense or follow facts and evidence to clear an officer of any wrongdoing. Shelby's reason for shooting Crutcher indicates that she is a danger to the public or the African American public. She stated: "…she fired her weapon out of fear because she said he didn't obey her command to lie on the ground…" One must wonder as to what caused her fear. The video showed Crutcher walking a distance in front of her with both hands in the air. If this posture created fear in her, then the entire public is suspect. What was she afraid of that caused her to shoot? She said that it was when he "appeared to reach inside his SUV for what she thought was a gun." The report noted that Crutcher was unarmed, the window as up, and no weapon was found in his SUV.

In the article, "Jury finds Tulsa officer not guilty," (The Oklahoman 5/18/2017) stated the following: "Prosecutors told jurors that Shelby overreacted. They noted Crutcher had his hands in the air and wasn't combative—part of which was confirmed by police video taken from a dashboard camera and helicopter that showed Crutcher walking away from Shelby, hands held above his head." We should note that Shelby was not alone on the scene; she had a fellow police officer near to her. One wonders what caused the jury to rule the way they did in view of all the visual information available to them.

In addition to being afraid, we learn that "Shelby also said she feared the influence of PCP, a powerful hallucinogenic known as Angel Dust that makes users erratic, unpredictable and combative." However, as stated earlier, Crutcher manifested none of those characteristics." After an autopsy was performed, PCP was found in his system and in his SUV. That information was discovered after the shooting, not before. One concern about this incident is why was Crutcher stopped? Could a force less lethal have been employed to effect Shelby's purpose? What kind of instructions was the jury given in their deliberation in this case?

Evidently, while the questions posed are important for the victim's family, they are seemingly meaningless to the jury when a police officer is involved. Our criminal justice system must be changed to one that acknowledges and respect the rights of all citizens, regardless of what they look like. The system also needs to reflect the fact that all police officers are not perfect and that they should experience repercussions for their misdeeds. As it stands today, an African American's words have no value against that of a police officer. He is always presumed guilty until proven innocent. The reason for that presumption is due to the system of European American supremacy and African American inferiority, the social conditioning European Americans receive in America from birth— African Americans and people of color are to be feared; they are viewed as dangerous and to be suspect. When a European American becomes a police officer, that social conditioning does not change. So, when Shelby said she was afraid of Crutcher, she was not lying, and the members of the jury identified with her and that fear. So, if that is the case, then where is the justice for the African Americans?

When the statement was made earlier that African Americans lose all their rights when stopped by a police officer was made, it was not based on conjecture, but facts and evidence. All one has to do is look at the litany of cases where an unarmed African American or person of color has been shot and killed when alternative uses of force were available. The fact that the Tulsa jury overlooked justice in this case underscores the need to replace the criminal justice system in America. People need to join in with groups who are working to change the system and do whatever is necessary (protest, petition, run for office, support organizations) to help effect change.

Fear is not a monopoly of European American police officers, because communities, family, friends of African Americans and other people of color experience it also, every time they are stopped by a police officer. Fear should never be the reality because the responsibility of all Americans is to ensure life, liberty, and justice for all. We have a lot of work to do; let us get to it.

Mesa, Arizona, and the Police Beatings of People of Color Go On and On

June 8, 2018

Four Mesa, Arizona police officers have been placed on paid leave while an investigation into their use of excessive force against an unarmed African American is being conducted. Fortunately, a video of the incident was available, so viewers could see for themselves what took place. Apparently, someone from an apartment building called the police to report a disturbance at that location. A young African American man, Robert Johnson, was waiting for an elevator and talking on his cell phone when he was approached by several police officers. Without any conversation, they began to frisk him, and then apparently, ordered the young man to move to another location away from the elevator, which he did while continuing to talk on his phone. Once he moved to the location where he had been ordered by the officer, he was then ordered to sit on the floor. Showing some hesitation in sliding down the wall to the floor, several officers began punching him in the face. Since he was leaning against the wall, he could not fall freely to the floor, so an officer bent down and pulled his legs out from under him at which time he landed on the floor. The officers continued to beat him until his hands were secured behind him. At no time did he offer any resistance.

The old saying that "a picture is worth a thousand words" could easily apply here in that the conduct of the officers was in question from the very beginning. Not once before the officer began their assault on the young man did they attempt to engage him in a civil conversation. Their attitude was seemingly that of a big bully that demanded immediate action when an order was given. The officers apparently had a perceived notion to enter into an altercation with the young man since they wasted no time in initiating their punches. At no time did any of the other officers present seek to stop the assault or advise the officers of their conduct relative to their actions. So, what do these pictures tell us about some police officers?

One of the first things this video tells us about these officers is that they have no respect for the young African American man. He was not treated respectfully like citizens should expect to be treated if they are minding their own affairs and causing attention to themselves. They showed a total disregard for his Constitutional rights by beginning their search of his body for something without cause. Johnson had no weapons, only a cell phone. The officers next used their authority as bullies to order Johnson to a wall on the opposite side of the area while still not informing him of anything that he did or was suspected of doing. Since he was surrounded by four fully armed and anxious officers, Johnson readily complied with the officers' order to move. As soon as he removed his cell phone from his ear, the beating began.

We might ask the question of why the police officers acted towards Johnson in this type of aggressive manner. They knew that Johnson poised no problem of violence or having a weapon on him after they searched him, and he complied with their orders. Yet, the officers felt that they were well within their rights to beat an unarmed man for no reason except for the fact that he was a person of color. One thing is certain from the actions of the officers, and that is reason played no part in their decision to beat Johnson. We know from many past similar experiences that the excuses of being afraid for their lives or feeling threatened or not being respected or obeyed were used to justify their actions. A simple answer to why they use excessive force and murder against people of color is because they do not consider them to be human beings.

We might also ask the question of why society in general is not outraged by the repeated unacceptable actions of these police officers against people of color. Could it be that they also do not see people of color as human beings? One reason for our making that assumption rests on the history of the repercussions experienced by many of the officers who committed atrocious acts against people of color. We would be incorrect in labeling the treatment many of the officers received for the actions as repercussions. The four officers from the Mesa Police Department were placed on paid leave. In other words, they received a paid vacation for their efforts, but no negative consequences. In the case of Betty Shelby, the female Tulsa, Oklahoma officer who shot and killed Terrance Crutcher in the back while he was walking away from her, after her department's report stated that she should not be allowed to serve as an officer dealing with the public, she was given a job in a city a few miles north of Tulsa. She was recently featured in a newspaper article where she had received a promotion and now offers classes to teach officers how to beat charges of abuse and excessive force. The list of officers not being held responsible for their misdeeds is too long to include here.

While the general American public remains silent relative to these officers' display of abuse of people of color accompanied with a chevalier attitude, they do not seem to realize that although the officers do not have to assume responsibility for their actions, the citizens for whom the officers work must pay large settlement payments to the victims and/or their families. The ethnic demographics are rapidly changing the makeup of American society and with those changes will come the need to redirect the focus and objectives of law enforcement. Some departments are making changes now because they understand that the amount of money being paid for officer's mistakes could be put to better use in educating them to treat all citizens fairly.

We have not seen the last video of police abuse of unarmed African American citizens simply because the system does not require them to take responsibility for their actions. The system must be replaced.

The Jury's Not Guilty Verdict of the Philando Castile Case Sent a Message to America

June 20, 2017

With the jury's finding of not guilty for the officer who killed Philando Castile comes the implied, but a blatant statement from law enforcement that the justice system overwhelmingly favors their agents—the police. The ruling says that in spite of you forcing us to use dash cams, body cams, and surveillance cams, you, the people, **cannot prevail over us because justice is what we say it is.** Most people of sound mind can usually tell right from wrong, but somehow lawyers, prosecutors, judges, district attorneys and others in the justice system cannot when a member of law enforcement is involved. We the people cannot continue to allow this miscarriage of justice to take place and assume that all is right with the world because it is not. So, what can the people do to replace his misguided system?

Although a disproportionate number of police victims have been people of color, the corruption is not exclusive to people of color, so, all people who want justice to serve everyone should be concerned and involved in bringing about a system that serves everyone. We know that many people are angry and concerned about the lack of justice simply by looking at the makeup of the protesters. While the protests serve a purpose in bringing the problems to public awareness, it should also serve as an opportunity to organize groups to study and develop plans of actions directed at replacing the system. Nothing will happen to replace the system if the people do not get involved and execute specific plans of actions. Also, change will not happen overnight.

The first order of business is to organize and develop a plan of approach to addressing the problem. The need for this process is important because it saves time and energy. For example, developing a plan to replace the chief of police, if effective, might bring about some relief, but would not solve the problem because the chief is simply one part of the total organization. Any plan to be effective must understand the system and its organizational structure in order to replace it completely. Some of the tools available to the people include **political power**—finding suitable candidates for the various offices and supporting them to victory; **political pressure**—the people putting pressure on current politicians to introduce legislation written to address many of the current problems in the justice system; **the law**—suing the city, police, Fraternal Order of the Police for as much money as possible so they get the message that injustice also comes with a price. Whatever approach taken must involve all concerned citizens, not just the vocal ones, and it must start at the local level.

We have heard all the excuses offered by law enforcement to justify their actions; excuses like "I felt threatened," or "I felt my life was in danger," or "I thought he was going for his gun," or "I was afraid for my life." All of these excuses and others have been offered as reasons for using deadly force, and yet, in spite of their fears and feelings of trepidations, many of these officers remain on the force. If they are in a state of constant fear or insecure feelings, they should not be in law enforcement. How can they "serve and protect" when they are under constant stress?

In addition to the individual excuses we hear the all too often references to the "bad apples" in the department or the "need for more training," or "the need for more officers," or "our lives are on the line every day." While all those reasons might be valid in some cases, none of the excuses explains why departments do not do a better job of vetting future officers or explain why some officers think it is fine to knowingly use excessive force, or officers using common sense and a degree of patience before resorting to deadly force, or spend more time educating departments and officers on the meaning of all people living in a diverse society rather than training in military combat tactics. Enough with all the excuses; ways and actions speak louder than words ever will.

We, the people, are tired of the unjust actions of the criminal justice system and its agents as well as the over-used excuses to try to justify and maintain the system. We are not trying to appeal to a sense of Christian fellowship or valuing our common humanity or democratic principles when we protest and ask for fairness for ourselves and fellow citizens, but to human decency and to a simple attempt to know the difference between right and wrong, and to seek to do what is right.

We should not take lightly the necessity for change in the system of justice as it continues to wreak havoc on the lives of people of color in general and show disregard for the rights of many of its citizens. To seek a replacement of the unjust system is not a suggestion, but a responsibility as noted in the Declaration of Independence: "But when a long train of abuses and usurpations, pursuing invariably the same object evinces a design to reduce them under absolute despotism, it is their right, it is their duty, to throw off such government, and to provide new guards for their future security." The founding fathers believed that replacing a corrupt and abusive system was not simply a choice but a "duty" of the people. The focus is not replacing the government, but the abusive system. We should not look to violence as part of a remedy for injustices, but the legal tools that are available and most of all, the people.

Change and replacement of the criminal justice system will not come easy or quickly because of the long years of its entrenchment, but it must come. Any plan for replacement must begin at the local level and involve as many people possible—strength in numbers. People wanting to join in the effort should look for groups and/or organizations already active in the process. Joining efforts with other individuals and organizations does not mean one has to agree with everything the group or organization represents but agreeing on replacing the justice system should be the primary focus.

The Starbucks Incident Involving the Arrest of Two African American Men Shows the Need for Implicit Education as well as Training

April 16, 2018

The recent arrest of two African American males at a Starbucks coffee shop in Philadelphia by police for no apparent reason has generated a plethora of questions regarding cultural bias and social justice. The situations, from media reports, involved two African American men who went to this Starbucks store to meet with someone. They apparently arrived before the party with whom they were to meet and so decided to sit and wait for their party. They asked to use the bathroom but were told by the employees that they could not use it because they had not purchased anything. At some point afterward, they were asked by the employees to leave, but they refused.

The reports noted that a statement from the Philadelphia Police Department Commissioner Richard Ross confirmed: "that on Thursday afternoon at 4:40 p.m., Philadelphia police received a 911 call from the

Starbucks at 18th and Spruce Streets alleging disturbance and trespassing." The two men were arrested, handcuffed, and taken to jail where they were placed in a holding cage for approximately eight hours, then released. No charges were made against them. A number of the people in the store at the time made known to the officers that the men were doing nothing wrong.

Fortunately, the men were unarmed and cooperated with the police or the outcome of the incident could have been tragic owning to the experiences of other men of color interacting with police officers. However, the primary question is why were they arrested, cuffed, and taken to jail in the first place? We cannot be certain of the specific reasons, but we can certainly address some possibilities that led to the incident. One reason has to do with implicit cultural bias. The person who called 911 and informed the police that the two men were creating a disturbance and trespassing did so because of the perception and judgment of the men. Perhaps men of color did not frequent that particular Starbucks, so their presence was unusual for the caller to experience. So, their presence in the store created in her a sense of fear.

After the incident, both Philadelphia's mayor and the police Commissioner made statements relative to their concerns about the incident. The Commissioner commented that his officers did nothing wrong; they simply followed orders requested by Starbucks. He also underscored the point that all his commanders received implicit bias training. He also stated that all the new recruits visit both the National Museum of African American History and Culture and the Holocaust Memorial Museum in Washington, D.C. The visits to these museums are supposed to show the recruits ethnic atrocities committed by policing

The mayor commented that seeing the headlines of the Starbucks incident in the headlines was disheartening to him and the incident "appears to exemplify what racial discrimination looks like in 2018." He also suggested that Starbucks' apology was not enough to satisfy his concerns about the incident and that he would look into whether the employees at Starbucks' should receive more implicit bias training.

The one key phrase used by both the Commissioner and the Mayor was "implicit bias training." To be sure, training is necessary when developing a skill is important, but what is more important and should come before the training is education. Both training and education are parts of the learning experience. However, most of the research over the last decade and longer indicate that people in general only have conscious access to 5 percent of our brains and that much of our brain's work happens on the unconscious level. In other words, when implicit bias occurs, that does not mean that people are hiding their ethnic and cultural biases; in essence, they do not know they have these biases.

Training helps to develop skills while education helps one to understand the skills and how they should be implemented. Training officers, as well as people in general, might help them do their job in some aspect of human relations, but education is needed for them to understand the presence of implicit cultural biases in their perceptions of people. So, the reference to officers and employees receiving more implicit training seems to be counterproductive if the objective is for them to be cognizant of what they are doing when they are doing it.

An example of implicit bias might serve to underscore the point of training and education relative to implicit bias training. An incident occurred a year or so ago where an inmate from a medical facility had left the grounds and was sitting in the middle of the street playing with some object. Someone called 911 and the police arrived. When the attendant who was also in the street talking to the inmate saw the police, he lies on his back and put both hands in the air to show he was not armed or represented a threat to the officers. When an officer approached him with his gun drawn, the attended told him that he worked at the facility and was presently trying to talk the inmate back onto the facility grounds. The European American officer shot the African American attendant in the leg. When the attendant asked the officer why he shot him since he had no weapon and represented to threat to him, the officer answered, "I don't know." We might assume that the officer was not thinking but simply reacted to the bias common among European American law officers—a fear of African American males.

While we appreciate and applaud the efforts of the Philadelphia Mayor and Police Commissioner relative to the need for implicit bias training, what we feel is more important in addition to the training is implicit bias education. All human beings have biases and prejudices, implicit as well as explicit, but the implicit ones are often unknown to them. With education, they have the opportunity to learn why the training is so important for them and all concerned. First, a bias must be discovered, then embraced, and overcome before success can be achieved. Training to overcome an unperceived bias is wasted time and effort. The officers who viewed the ethnic museums must learn that the experience was not entertainment, but lessons that underscore the fact that we are all implicated in the actions of all human beings.

Why European Americans call 911 When They See People of Color

May 14, 2018

The recent rash of incidents involving European Americans calling the police after seeing African Americans doing something they thought suspect should come as no surprise based on the ethnically biased social conditioning that is a part of their everyday American life experience.

The very first element of a European Americans life experience is the idea that they and all people who look like they look are the centers of the universe. From their skin complexion to their standards and values, society leads them to see themselves as superior to all people not like them. Everything in their immediate environment serves to support that concept. As their social environment begins to expand from the home to the neighborhood, church, and school, they are made to realize that they have privileges over people who are not like them. The awareness of their specialness begins in the home where little if any interactions with people of color take place, but often negative references, actions, and reactions are observed as a normal part of their daily experiences.

The European American lady at Starbuck, the lady at Yale, the lady who saw the three African American women leaving the Airbnb all felt within their rights to call the police because they witnessed something their social conditioning told them was not normal. Apparently, none of these European American women gave any thought to their action before calling the police. Because of their conditioning relative to fear and danger associated with people of color, the primary thing to trigger their concern was the skin color of the people representing the threat to their sense of normalcy. I.e., ethnic bias against people of color by European Americans is triggered by skin color.

A European American female called the police when she observed an African American female asleep in her dorm's common room. The student, a graduate student at Yale was awakened when the European American female told her she had no right to sleep there. The reason the European American female called the police was that of the fear and dread she felt by seeing a person of color in a place that was usually reserved, in the female's mind, for European Americans. The brown color of the graduate student's complexion sent a warning signal to the brain of the European American female, so she acted on it without any serious consideration regarding repercussions. She evidently felt unsafe in her home environment with a person of color present.

A European American female in Rialto, California called police when she thought several African American women who were leaving an Airbnb rental looked out of place. That is, she thought it unusual for women of color to be in that neighborhood. When she noticed that they were loading baggage into a vehicle, she assumed that they were burglars. Shortly after the 911 call was made several police cars arrived on the scene. In addition, a helicopter flew overhead while the women were being questioned. Once again, the biased social conditioning this woman received relative to skin color helped to trigger her response to people of color being where she did not expect them to be by calling 911.

In both incidents, the social conditioning of cultural biases played a significant role in the actions of the three European American females involved. Little or no thoughts were given to the well-fair of the African Americans because their social value was never in question. In each situation, the European American female seemingly believed seeing African Americans in the settings they were in was not normal. So, the automatic response was to call the police and have the discomfort removed.

The ethnic bias of the European American females was reinforced by the police who arrived on the scene already favoring the callers. The rights of the African Americans are immediately suspect as noted in the actions of the police officers and their immediate treatment of the African

Americans. Rather than taking the time to assess the situation prior to any detaining or arresting actions, the police arrived on the scene already suspecting the African Americans of wrongdoings. The complicit police actions supported the biases of the European American females toward the African Americans.

Comments emanating from the police establishment of the three incidents mentioned above all suggest that the police were simply doing their jobs. Yes, they were doing their jobs, but only in support of the European American callers. The rights of the African American men and women were given little or no preference equal to that of the callers. The actions of the police seem to suggest that a call 911 is taken as fact without question, so doing their job means not giving the African American citizens involved their respect, rights or privileges. Many European Americans, as well as many police officer do not realize that America is a diverse society.

Because many European Americans live with an ethnic bias of which they are not cognizant, or their biases are implicit, the first order of business in replacing that bias is discovering that they have a cultural bias against people of color. Next, they need to confront their bias with the thought of replacing it with a more appropriate concept of a diverse humanity. Finally, once they know their bias and know how it is triggered, they can work towards overcoming it. While all Americans can address their bias using this process, European American in positions involving serving the public must certainly experience this form of education.

The problem of cultural ethnic bias as a part of social conditioning cannot be resolved easily or quickly because it involves commitment, discipline, and consistency. All three steps must be followed if success is to occur. Once we understand that bigotry is a part of a system, we will realize that biases do not exist in isolation, but they must be replaced individually.

Ethnic Bigotry on the Judicial Bench—A Case in Point

May 3, 2017

Many Americans believe that as a society we have made tremendous progress in our acceptance of one another as equals regardless of our skin color. Although we would like to believe this, the fact of the matter is that ethnic bigotry permeates the whole of American society in the system of European American (white) supremacy. In many cases, the bigotry is subtle and often passes for ignorance or innocence. At other times, the bigotry is so apparent; it cannot be excused with some form of rationale. One of the features of European American supremacy is expressed in an attitude of superiority over the ideas, opinions, and statements of people of color, especially African Americans. A case in point occurred recently in an article by Randy Ellis, in *The Oklahoman,* "Black judge: Repeating 'n' word in appellate opinion was 'unnecessary.' (4/29/2017)

According to the article, the only African American judge on the Oklahoma Court of Criminal Appeals, Vice Presiding Judge David Lewis, made the statement regarding his fellow judge's opinion: "I concur in the decision reached by the court in this matter. However, I write separately to point out that the author of this opinion did not have to repeat the repugnant language used by the appellant." Lewis' words to his colleague, Judge Gary Lumpkin, were to alert him to the sensitivity of the word to him, and indeed to the public, and that he found its frequent repetition unnecessary. Lewis wrote that "The repeated use of the 'n' word in this opinion was unnecessary to the reader's understanding of the language used by the appellant, and unnecessary to the court's resolution of this case."

In many cases like this one, the judge receiving comments of this nature would recognize the lack of sensitivity shown in his or her case and offer an apology for the offense and a "thank you" for the cautionary note from the colleague. One would think that a judge on the bench today would be fully apprised of the sensitive nature of the 'n' word. The article noted that: "Judge Lumpkin quoted the racial slur verbatim in his opinion, while Lewis used the euphemistic expression 'n' word in his criticism."

What followed, according to the article, underscored the apparent ethnic bigotry that exists not only in society but also on the bench: "Robert Hudson, another judge on the court, defended Lumpkin's decision to quote the racial slur." Rather than accepting Lewis' words to Lumpkin as a form of "corrective criticism," and an appeal to his better judgment, Hudson interpreted Lewis' comments as an affront to Lumpkin's judgment and continued "Our cases reflect reality and that reality is oftentimes not pretty." In other words, Hudson seems to imply that one reality trumps another reality; in this case, the reference to an African American slur word, which could have easily been avoided, should be used regardless of its offensiveness to his fellow judge and society. The question is why would a judge continue to use an offensive ethnic slur word when he knows that it can easily be avoided. European American arrogance?

Robert Hudson excused Lumpkin's use of the 'n' word by noting that: "…if we are willing to erase highly relevant—albeit offensive—facts from our opinions, we will send a terrible message to the bench, bar and public that the truth, when objectionable, should be redacted merely to avoid controversy." Hudson tried to use aspects of the case to make his point, but it fails on the history of prior court practices. The details of a sexual attack perpetrated on some young female would be not reused time and again verbatim if the judge knew that the language was sensitive to her and the court.

The point relative to this article focuses more on the attitude and actions of the two European American judges rather than the actual case. For example, if the three judges were having lunch together, and one of the European American judges started to tell an offensive ethnic joke and the African American judge stopped him and asked that he not tell the joke in his presence because he found it to be offensive, common sense dedicates that a reasonable person would acquiesce and not tell the joke. However, if the other European American judge wanted to hear the joke and encouraged the teller of the joke to continue, we would realize that he had no regards for the feelings of his African America colleague. In addition, he showed disrespect by his actions, and that his selfish desire was more important than his colleague's feelings and request. The African American's request was that the joke not be told in his presence, not that it not be told at all.

The system of European American (white) supremacy has conditioned the European Americans to view African Americans and other people of color as inferior regardless of their social, economic, educational, political and judicial status. That system causes European Americans to view reality through a warped sense of value. For example, when the topic of race is ever brought into a conversation, the European American rarely thinks of him or herself as being part of a race. They have been falsely conditioned to view themselves as representatives of the human race—everyone else belongs to a different race. In addition, they see themselves as being the center of the universe and in control of society.

So, when Lewis, the African American judge said to his colleague that he found the repetition of the 'n' word to be excessive and unnecessary to the case, Hudson, a European American judge, and colleague of both Lumpkin and Lewis took exception to Lewis' comments. Lewis had said previously that the repetition of the 'n' word verbatim had no direct bearing on the outcome of the case. Hudson used his sense of superiority to castigate Lewis for speaking the truth to his European colleague. So, Hudson had to put the African American judge in his "place" as an inferior. Hudson, seemingly, believed that his opinion regarding Limpkin's excessive use of the 'n' word over-ruled or trumped the opinion of Lewis for no other reason than he was European American.

Some people might think that these comments are simply making a mountain out of a molehill by suggesting that ethnic bigotry was at the core of Hudson's criticism of Lewis. When read carefully, the article noted that Lewis agreed with the finding of the case. He just felt the use of the 'n' word was excessive. Because of the socially biased conditioning of Hudson's and European Americans generally, their ability to relate to insensitive words or phrases directed at ethnic Americans of color are rarely perceived and understood. However, even large learning curves can be overcome with effort.

Law Enforcement Should Acknowledge Role in Historic Police Violence Regarding African Americans

July 22, 2016

One of the ironies concerning the recent instances of police shootings is the reaction of law enforcement regarding the shootings. The entire nation is put on alert and more arms are brought out in preparation for defense against the shooters. More officers are brought out into the field or on the streets as if there was going to be a war-like conflict between the police shooters and the police. What we find in looking at the individuals who shoot police is that they generally acted alone. When attempting to answer the question of why the police were attacked, the police never say that maybe they had something to do with instigating the violence. And that is the irony.

For approximately three-hundred-years, law enforcers have shown little respect to people of color as they abused, assaulted, exploited, and killed them. The concern for justice and fairness was never an issue in the years before civil rights. Whatever the law enforcers wanted to do, they do with impunity. The victims of color had no one or place to turn to for justice or fairness when the perpetrators were the law enforcers who were supposed to protect them. Most complaints to others in authority fell on deaf ears, and usually, nothing was done. At the same time, an African American or person of color person could be accused of committing a crime and be sent to prison or death without even a semblance of a fair or just trial. If we were to check the records of violence and lynching's committed against African Americans in police custody over the past few decades, we would not receive accurate data because the law enforcers did not record it or would not want to appear like they had a part in creating the data.

Today, with the advance of technology the world is able to witness the behavior of some law enforcers as they interact with people of color. In many cases, what is seen does not usually coincide with what the officer says happened. However, regardless of what is seen on the videos, the officers usually experience little if any repercussions for their involvement. For many of the people who watch the videos, justice or fairness does not seem to serve the African Americans. One reason offered by former and current police officers in trying to explain the behavior of European American police officers is fear of the African American man. Norm Stamper, the author of *Breaking Rank*, noted that "From the earliest days of academy training it was made clear that black men and white cops don't mix, that of all the people we'd encounter on the streets, those most dangerous to our safety, to our survival, were black men." If we are to take these words of a former police officer as truth, then we can readily understand why the European American police officer fears African American men—their safety and survival.

From where did that threat of safety and survival come relative to the European American officer? One possibility might come from the bigotry present in the social conditioning of European Americans. Whether that fear is real or imaginary, the mere fact that it is announced in the academy or is common knowledge in the departments, it can serve as an excuse for officers to use the threat of death as a defense to shoot, beat or other abusive activity of African Americans. To underscore this point, Stamper stated: "Simply put, white cops are afraid of black men. We don't talk about it, we pretend it doesn't exist, we claim 'color blindness,' we say white officers treat black men the same way they treat white men. But that's a lie." Why has the public been kept in the dark about this fear? Maybe because keeping it secret serves a useful purpose for some people.

When a police officer is killed in the line of duty, brother and sister officers from all over the nation attend the funeral to pay their respects and show support for their members. Often huge processions and motorcades become part of the ceremony celebrating the service of the fallen officer. We all feel the loss and mourn with the family because every life is important and valued. We understand and appreciate the feelings of tribalism is the thin blue line. What we Americans find difficult to understand, however, is when a twelve-year-old boy playing with a toy gun alone in a public park is shot by an officer there is no-show of concern from the police department or the "good "officers on the force. The first utterance from the law enforcement agencies is usually the "officer had probable cause." Little else is said.

No person in his or her healthy mind wants or wishes the death of another human being. However, if an individual has witnessed years of injustices, miscarriage of the law, abuse, assaults, and death to people who share the same identity but different skin color, but realize no sense of justice or concern for justice by the very people who volunteer their lives to serve and protect them, his or her sense of reality can be altered. Law enforcement agencies need to examine themselves to learn what part they play in creating the fear and behavior that contributes to the deaths of many men of color and subsequently to the death of their fellow officers.

Just recently a young African American man, Charles Kinsey, a physical therapist was attempting to render service to a young male autistic patient who was sitting in the middle of the street playing with a toy truck. Someone called the police and said someone was in the street with a gun. When Kinsey realized the police were on the scene, he laid on his back with both hands in the air and shouted loud to the police not to shoot. He told them that he was a therapist and the young man was autistic so please do not shoot. Totally disregarding what the therapist said, one of the officers shot Kinsey, made him turn over and handcuffed him. The irony of this case is that the autistic man was European American and had the object in his hand. The therapist was on his back with both hands in the air, yet he was the one the police shot with a rifle, not a gun.

Later, when the officer was asked why he shot Kinsey, his reply was "I don't know." Is there any wonder why some people lose their perspective about the police? Things must change for the better for all Americans, but especially for African Americans. Some members of the FOP are quick to claim that anyone who says something negative about police behavior is totally anti-police, but that is not true. People can be pro-police but find fault in some police behavior. For the FOP to put all the blame of police misconduct on a few "bad officers" is faulty logic. If a pack of dogs is charging towards a person with mouths open, teeth glaring, tongues salivating, how is he supposed to select the ones who will not bite him? This example is not meant as disrespect to officers, but when they all act in concert, how can the good ones be distinguished from the bad ones? The police need to start accepting some responsibility for the violence committed against people of color and make appropriate changes.

The problems relative to the shooting of African Americans and police is not reserved to those two entities, but to all America. We need to address the problems now.

THE BIGGER PICTURE

Part III

"The improvement of understanding is for two ends:
first, our own increase of knowledge; secondly, to
enable us to deliver that knowledge to others."
~ John Locke

Race is Being Replaced by Ethnic Group and Ethnicity to Eliminate Confusion

February 14, 2017

When the founding fathers invented the system of European American (white) supremacy and African American (black) inferiority their basic mistake was to base their system on race by color. If they controlled society, they controlled the system, but they could not control the color of each group or the fact that we humans belong to one species of Homo sapiens. Time would eventually debunk the myth of race and begin to deconstruct the social conditioning forced on society. Many Americans are still today confused relative to the difference between race and ethnicity. Much of the confusion was caused by the scientist who wanted to push their own theories about race since it has never been defined socially. Even the term "white" experienced several transitions in its application to various immigrant groups to America—examples of Anglo-Saxon whites, free whites, lesser whites, and Caucasians were common. All these groups, including people of color, were considered ethnic groups, except the Anglo-Saxons.

With all the demographic changes taking place in America and the world today, a clear understanding of the terms race and ethnicity is in order. We began by stating that all human belongs belong to one race.

What we commonly refer to as races today simply does not exist. We are all of one blood. The differences we experience in others come from our cultures and places of habitation. Those differences represent our ethnic differences and have nothing to do with race. The problem has been that we use race to mean ethnicity or confuse something purely cultural with something we think is biological. According to Bill Nye, author of *Undeniable*, (2014) "In evolutionary terms or fact, we are all almost identical. We each share 99.9 percent of the same DNA."

All our social identities are based on either our cultural and/or geographical attachments; one or the other or a combination of both geography and culture represent the ethnic identity. People from countries like China or India will have their culture included in the country's name. The name of the country usually serves as the person's ethnic identity if that country is the one of his or her birth. If, however, the parents of the person are known for their cultural identity, for example, American Indian, then the cultural identity serves as the ethnic identity. Because of these two influences, all people have two separate and often distinct identities—one ancestral or ethnic, and one cultural.

An example is in order here: If a Russian male and an Iranian female marries and have a child, that child will have an ancestral (ethnic) identity that includes both Russian and Iranian parents. However, depending on the country in which the parents are living, their child's cultural identity might be totally different from the parents. That is, if the family is living in Iran, then the child' cultural identity will, unless certain circumstances prevent it, reflect that country and culture. If for example, the couple lived in America, the child's cultural identity would be American. At some point in the child's life, a choice of a parent's ethnic identity might be embraced. The child's cultural identity of American will remain unless and until it is relinquished.

Another way of viewing ethnicity is by looking at the identities of the diverse people who come to America. No one comes to America legally with an identity where color is stipulated, only the geographical identity which often includes the cultural identity. For example, many professional athletes from foreign countries come to work in America and regardless of their ethnic and/or ancestral identity, are identified by their geographical identity. For example, the following professional basketball players of brown complexions, are simply called Brazilians: Nene, Anderson Varejao, Tiago Splitter, Lucas Nogueira, Bruno Caboclo, and Leandro Barbosa. Two players from Australia, Kyrie Irving and Patty Mills, players with brown complexions, are known as Australians, not by their ethnic identities, but by geographical (cultural) ones. That is not to suggest that their ancestral identities are not important to them, they are not necessary to underscore their cultural identities.

Because our founding fathers instituted the system of supremacy and forced the social conditioning on all Americans, race has been at the core of all social challenges. All the social biases Americans of color experience today are based on race. Now that society is starting to understand the confusion caused by race by color and is working to replace the system of bigotry, not knowing what to do about race is a problem. We know that race is an illusion, but one that we have been living with since the beginning of our society. As race continues to lose its social value, it must be replaced with something and that something is ethnic and cultural identities. Ethnic identities were and are important in collecting data, so society and the government can monitor what is taking place relative to the general population and each ethnic group. The U.S. Census began in 1790 was a way to maintain and control the population, especially the ethnic groups of color. The changing demographics in our world and society continue to blur the lines of race as an acceptable term suitable for social identities.

Today, if each group is identified by ethnicity rather than race, discrimination by race would no longer possible. As society pushes through this process of change from racial identities to ethnic ones, we must recognize that arriving at ethnic identities is just a temporary pause, because the result, in an idealistic sense, is having a need for no other identity than American.

The primary reason for some Americans to identify themselves as European American, African American, and Asian Americans etc.... comes from a lack of information about their countries of origin. The results are seen in the terms European, African, Hispanic, etc.... that rely on either geography or culture to fill in that space before "American" for ethnicity identification. The over-all objective of identity in our democratic society is for everyone regardless of their ancestral, ethnic or cultural identities to be seen and known as Americans. Embracing, promoting, and being proud one's ethnic identity does not take away from the fact that America should value all ethnicities. Two facts remain—no one chooses his or her ancestral (ethnic) identity, and everyone can choose his or her cultural identity.

President Trump is Not a Racist, But He Seemingly Does Not Mind Being Called One

January 13, 2018

What strikes some Americans as interesting and humorous is the reaction to President Trump's bigoted remarks in general, but the recent remarks about countries of brown people. Trump has been a bigot all his life, so why would he change at this late date in his life. He would not and possibly could not because this bigotry was part of the normal flavor of his entire social environment.

Many people are asking the question: Is President Trump a racist? The answer is no; he is not a racist. Being called a racist for people with an ethnic bias towards people of color is not a criticism of them, but a compliment. The reason is simple. The term racist represents the view of a large group of people holding the same beliefs of a race by color or white (European American) supremacy and African American (black) inferiority. The term racist underscores the belief the group holds, so the label reasserts that bias belief. Since the term racist is a derivative of the word race, and the word race relative to the invention of a so-called black race and a white race is bogus, then the concept of individuals being racist, believing that the European Americans are superior is false although it is used as a part of the American parlance. So, what is President Trump if he is not a racist?

President Trump is a bigot and has been since his formative years in America. His bigotry was not something that was taught to him specifically but was a part of his social conditioning. What too many Americans fail to realize is that America is a bigoted society and has been since the founding fathers invented the system of European American supremacy. We do not have to guess about the truthfulness of this bigotry, all we need to do is look at the history of the African American experience is American and the challenges of the civil rights activists to verify the existence of bigotry. The problem that exists and notably with Trump is that the bigotry was obtained as a natural characteristic or feature of his social, private and public environment. That being the case, he as well as other Americans do not recognize the abuse, unjust, inhumane, and un-American treatment of African Americans and people of color as abnormal.

The social system under which Trump and many other European Americans grew-up under did not recognize African Americans and people of color as well as poor European American people as having any social value worthy of attention. So, for the most part, people of color became invisible to European Americans unless they were in daily contact with them. The contact, however, was often experienced as occurring between superior European Americans and inferior people of color.

The many negative stereotypes of not only African Americans but also people of color in other parts of the world prevailed in the bigoted American psyche. For example, the visual and mental descriptions of Africans as ignorant, barbaric, cannibals with bones in their hair, running around in circles half naked were deliberate and vile examples of ethnic bigotry. Nonetheless, those images and descriptions were taken as facts and incorporated into the mind of many European Americans like Trump. The results of these negative stereotypes of African Americans and people of color served to support the lack of social value afforded them by European Americans. The negative stereotypes were presented to American society in such a way that the European Americans, as well as some of the people of color, did not recognize the pictures that were being painted. One of the major influences of American bigotry was in the motion picture industry in that African Americans were not seen on the big screen except in rolls of servitude or villains.

The point here is that many of the European Americans today who say they are surprised and or offended by Trumps bigoted comments need to take a look at the society in which they live and when and where they have objected to the injustice, abuse, discrimination, and bigotry of African Americans and turned a blind eye, a deaf ear, and a closed mouth at what they observed. Many European Americans are hypocrites if anything about bigotry in society because they know it exists and chose to ignore it.

What is so disheartening about the situation in America today is that many reasonable, intelligent, patriotic Americans recognized the bigotry in Trump years ago but still do nothing but stand by and let the values, positive leadership and integrity of America slip by the wayside. No, Trump is not a racist, but many people will try and argue the point when nothing is to be gained from their efforts. Hardly anyone, it seems, is offended by being called a racist because that term identifies a member of a group, not simply an individual. However, when a person is called a bigot, they then must accept direct responsibility and defend themselves or admit to the charge. Either way, the biased mindset is not placed in a group, but the individual in question. That is why Trump is not a racist, but a bigot.

The recent derogatory remarks made by Trump regarding Haiti and Africa immigrants underscore the hypocrisy that exists not only in Congress but in society as well. Why was it only two of the six-plus senators had the courage to speak up and call the remarks offensive and biased? A probable answer is because the other senators saw nothing unusual or out of the ordinary about the comments. Even after word of the remarks had been made public the general reaction of some senators was like this was simply business, as usual, no need to get upset about what the President said.

Ethnic bigotry is a common fact in American life and little has affected many European Americans' view of African Americans and people of color. Fortunately, change continues to force glimmers of light and reality through the darkness of biased ignorance that tries to hold back progress. Time and change are on the side of light.

Good Community Relationships with the Police Requires Clear, Realistic Perception

January 29, 2018

In an article by Mark A. Yancey, "Police and community relationship goes 2 ways," (The Oklahoman 1/28/2017) his first two sentences underscore the reasons why community relationships need a lot of work. He stated that: "In the wake of recent police-involved shootings around the country, I often hear that police need to **rebuild** trust with the communities they serve. While I agree trust needs to be re-established, we should not place the entire burden of **restoring** trust, promoting respect and tolerance and following the law solely on the police." Two words are used in these sentences that demonstrate Yancey's lack of understanding of the problems involved with building a relationship with the communities; those two words are rebuild and restoring.

While we can applaud Yancey's desire to seek a good relationship with communities, we must recognize that he is a citizen of a society with a natural bias against people of color. Chances are, he does not realize his bias because it is not something he consciously acquired but was conditioned to be by society—his home, neighborhood, school, church, city, state, and nation. One example should suffice to show how the bias works. If an officer observes a nice-looking late-model car driven by a young African American male, chances are two thoughts will cross the officer's mind—the car is stolen, or the driver is a drug dealer. However, if the drive of the car is a young European American male, the two thoughts might be that he is a spoiled kid, or it is the family's car. The thoughts relative to the African American male were not made from malice or anger; they are conditioned responses. If the officer does not recognize the negative thoughts relative to the African American, then they cannot be replaced.

One cannot rebuild or restore relationships that never existed in the first place. The relationship the officer has with the communities is the one conditioned by a society which sees people of color in a negative context. The relationship should be for the officer to serve and protect all the citizens without bias, but when the bias is hidden by social convention, the lines get blurred.

Yancey's next sentence also underscored a problem of a lack of understanding in the police-community relationship: "Relationship-building, after all, is a two-way street and requires **mutual trust, respect,** and **tolerance**." When we stop and look at some of the recent videos of police treatment of young African American men, we recognize that all three of these elements are missing from the behavior of the officers. Officers are paid by the citizens to do their jobs; the citizens are not, so it is incumbent on the officers to serve as examples in these areas. History shows us that the law enforcement agency has been wanting in these three areas relative to their relationship with the African American community. For example, shortly after former President Obama had taken office, a noted scholar a professor from a prestigious university was arrested for entering his own home. He identified himself to the officer, told the officer that the home was his, and showed him the key to the door. The officer disregarded all the professor said and arrested him. What happened to trust, respect and tolerance during this experience?

Another recent example of where the police disregard these areas of trust, respect, and tolerance involved a young African American man who had used a tool to do some work on the sunroof of his car. Someone from the neighborhood called 911 and reported someone breaking into an auto. When the young man's car was pulled over, he got out with both hands in the air. The video showed the officers issuing orders and simultaneously charging the young man, not giving him any time to obey the commands. To add insult to injury, the officers kept telling the young man to stop resisting when there were three or four officers on him, pushing his face into the concrete, punching him and holding his hand behind his back with an officer's knee. Yet, they kept yelling at him to stop resisting—he was not resisting. How could he when he was face down on the pavement with three or four officers on him? Where were the respect and tolerance? Videos of both these incidents exist and the behavior of the officer/officers can be observed on **YouTube.**

Yancey mentioned that "citizens need to do their part in the rebuilding process by avoiding unnecessary, violent confrontations with officers." Officer Yancey would do well to review many of the videos that show no violence on the part of the citizens unless or until it is initiated by officers who are in a rush to subdue a citizen. The fact is that when an officer stops a citizen, the citizen loses all his or her rights because if a video and audio history of the event is not available, the law enforcement community will disregard anything the citizen has to say but accepts everything the officer has to say.

Time and again, videos have shown that citizens can observe the laws, and follow police orders and still get beaten, or shot, and then arrested. We are not saying that the citizens are never at fault; many times, they are, and many times mental illness has some part to play in the events. Yancey stated that "The law requires officers to respect the citizens they serve. Citizens should show police the same respect they rightfully demand by cooperating with officers' instructing and letting our judicial system resolve peacefully and disagreements about the lawfulness of their actions." In an ideal world Yancey's statement might be acceptable, but, if the citizen cannot present evidence to prove his or her case, it is an automatic win for the officer. All we need to do is check the record of police cases of misconduct and see how many convictions have been placed on the officers.

The first order of business in trying to establish good community relationships is for the police departments to understand their history with the community. If the elements of trust, respect, and tolerance are missing, then the first question should be why? Chances are the problems start with the biased perception of the citizens conditioned in the law enforcers by society. That is the first thing that needs to change—all citizens should be viewed as citizens, no differences. We can admire Yancey's efforts in wanting to address this problem, but he needs to better understand the role of the police officers and their relationship to the community before asking the community to give what must be earned—trust, respect, and tolerance.

Dialogues on Race Will Not Unite America, But Keep It Divided

July 15, 2016

Since the recent incidents in Louisiana, Minnesota, and Texas, where the lives of African Americans and European Americans have been lost, many protest marches across the country, many town hall meetings, and many talk shows have been conducted that focused on America being a divided country because of color—black and white. The objectives of all these activities are to somehow bring the country together harmoniously. Many recommendations and plans will be suggested, and some will be implemented to correct the recent and decades-old injustices committed against African Americans by European Americans. Unfortunately, all the plans, programs, and recommendations will be short-lived because we cannot be united until we learn and fix what keeps us divided. No problem based on race will ever be resolved talking about race—black and white. Every discussion that involves race can only go in a circle; we know circles have no ends.

To resolve a problem involving race we must get beyond race, i.e.…we must establish an approach to discussing the nature of the problem without invoking the concept of race because if we do not, then we accomplish nothing but a waste of time. Let us be specific in identifying the problem that keeps America divided. If we say the answer is race, we are partially correct because race is the key word. However, our acceptance of the concept of race is the problem. Ever since the founding fathers invented the concept of a black race and a white race, separate and unequal, we Americans have been living our lives based on a myth, a falsehood, and an invention. The problems we experience as a divided society today are all based on our acceptance of the false concept of race. The reason for the invention of races was control of the people, all the people. For European Americans, the concept of superiority was important and necessary to serve as a buffer between the slaves, the poor, and the élite. The invention was/ is known as the system of white supremacy and black inferiority.

The system of white supremacy does not exist in isolation but must have the component of black inferiority to complete its existence. Both terms are different sides of the same coin. The system of supremacy became the focus of social conditioning of the psyches of all Americans. For European Americans, according to Dr. Robin DiAngelo, a European American scholar, "We [European Americans/whites] have set the world up to preserve that internal sense of superiority and also resist challenges to it. All while denying that anything is going on and insisting that race is meaningless to us." In other words, the system of white supremacy was created to protect and perpetuate itself. She adds: "We have organized society to reproduce and reinforce our racial interest and perspectives. Further, we are centered in all matters deemed normal, universal, benign, neutral and good."

The founding fathers based their invention of races on the color of skin which was illogical as well as irrational because skin color is not a constant determinant of race. At the time the invention was instituted the founding fathers had control of society and the power to enforce their laws. The legacy of their invention relative to people of color, and African Americans, in general, was the elements of danger, anger, fear, and hatred. These negative elements relative to people of color were/are processed as natural and normal to the perception and understanding of European Americans. African Americans were forced to view themselves in public to conform to the perception of the biased European American views.

The actions of some members of law enforcement today underscore the retention of the beliefs that the system of Supremacy promoted. Our understanding of the system of white supremacy and how it influences our perceptions should tell us that any discussion involving race in society is tainted if the bias concept of white supremacy is not replaced. Too many European Americans view African Americans and people of color as inferior normally. Since that is the case, any idea of fairness and justice by these European Americans will be influenced by their ethnic bias, much of which they never realize or recognize because it has always been natural and normal to them. Unfortunately, when the European American's biased viewpoint is challenged, they can become offended because they think their sense of objectivity is being challenged.

The most challenging part of bringing together our divided country is replacing the concept of race and its lack of authenticity and reliability. A recent comment by Dorothy Roberts, a University of Pennsylvania professor, underscores the point. Race has never been defined with any consistency and Professor Roberts adds: "That's because race is based on cultural, legal, social and political determinations, and those groupings have changed over time. As a social scientist, looking at biologists treating these groupings as if they were determined by innate genetic distinctions, I'm dumbfounded. There's so much evidence that they're invented social categories. How you can say this is a biological race is just absurd. It's absurd. It violates the scientific evidence about human beings. "Unfortunately, many European Americans choose to hold on tightly to the myth.

If we can accept the factual information we know about race and supremacy, then any discussion that speaks to resolving problems concerning the concept of race must begin with a forthright rejection of a black and a white race, and the normal perception of the inferiority of people of color by European Americans. If those changes do not occur, then no reasonable and fair discussion can take place. Race cannot be a part of that discussion if race is assumed to be an acceptable and legal term. We must come to understand that what divides America is the illusion of race and racial differences. If we do not debunk those illusions, we have no basis from which to build a construction together. If we are going to solve the social problems that are the results of ethnic biases, we must do so as social equals.

Changing the Criminal Justice System and Mass Incarceration Starts at the Local Level

July 10, 2018

Often, when something happens involving the criminal justice system that has a negative effect on a segment of society, that part of society that is not seemingly directly impacted will pay little or no attention to the problem. Usually, they remain uninvolved and uninformed relative to the criminal justice until it affects them directly. What they do not realize is that they have always been directly affected by the system whether they know it or not. One way they, the public, is affected is through the high rate of incarceration and prison overcrowding that the citizens are financially responsible for paying. However, since they do not receive the bill directly, they give little attention to it. The groups that are forced to pay the bills are the poor and people of color. So, for many years mass incarceration has been about controlling people of color and the poor right in plain sight while nothing was done to correct the injustices that were committed against them.

Studies have been conducted relative to mass incarceration ascertaining that the phenomena are not simply an act of maintaining law and order, but a system of economic profit-making. Several scholars have referred to the criminal justice system as the prison industrial complex because of the vastness of the system and the many people involved at many different levels. Although this system is a nationwide organization, what keeps it going happens at the local levels of society. So, if an effort is made to replace the unjust system, the initial action must take place at the local level. The first order of business is to re-educate the public and present a transparent picture of what happens to a citizen that is incarcerated at the local level and how he or she becomes part of the bodies working for the system.

Many citizens are led to believe that because a person is arrested, charged, and sent to prison that they deserve to be there because they broke the law. Generally speaking, that would be an accurate assessment. However, what created the present situation of mass incarceration had nothing to do with citizens breaking the law, but with the laws being changed to expand the number of people being incarcerated. When President Reagan instituted his war on drugs and crime, he caused a modification of the charges and length of sentencing. The system has since added the fees, fines, and numerous charges to the sentence of the incarcerated person, making freedom almost impossibility if one happens to be poor or a person of color. So, the more people introduced into the system, the more efficiently it runs. For an in-depth look at the subject of mass incarceration please read Michelle Alexander's book THE NEW JIM CROW.

The state of Oklahoma is one of the national leaders regarding mass incarceration in general, but number one as far as incarcerating women is concerned. This problem was brought to the attention of the Oklahoma citizens in the form of two state questions that addressed the rate of incarceration of people with drug problems and non-violent crimes. The state passed the two questions 780 and 781 that sought to reclassify drug possession and some other lower-level crimes as misdemeanors. The objective of the questions was to use the money saved from not incarcerating people of these types of crimes and use that money for alternative programs. These types of programs are necessary for addressing the problems and redirecting the money.

Kris Steele, a former Speaker of the House, is the chairman of Oklahomans for Criminal Justice Reform and leader in attempting to stop the mass march to prison of many citizens. Based on his studies and experiences relative to criminology he understands that prison is not the answer to problems involving drug use and low-level offenses. He expressed some of his concerns in an article, "Justice reform must have buy-in," (7/9/2018) that underscored the injustice of the sentencing today. He also noted the importance of the people involved in the working of the criminal justice system understanding the problems and helping to overcome many of these problems, not trying to maintain the status quo. Steele noted the need for elected officials and others to accept the programs. He stated that "Unfortunately, some elected officials still haven't accepted this approach. In the six months after the state questions were enacted, 882 people were sent to prison with drug possession as their most serious offense—directly rebutting the will of voters."

One of the problems in this matter is the lack of concern of many of the citizens; they either do not care or do not know the seriousness of mass incarceration. Steele noted that citizens pay the price and it is significant: "If each of these 882 people sentenced to prison for drug possession spent one year in prison, it would cost the taxpayer $15 million, and if they were imprisoned for the statewide average for drug possession—25 months—it would cost $32 million.

We know that mass incarceration is a feature of the criminal justice that keeps the system going; we also know that the system is unjust and unfair to people of color and the poor. We realize that we can start to resolve the problem if we work together. Steele noted that "Once this cultural change is embraced by those responsible for implementing reform, Oklahoma can safely reduce its incarceration rate, boost public safety and strengthen families." Oklahomans must keep the pressure for corrective action open and out front for change to occur.

Along with addressing the problem of mass incarceration is the need for prison reform from a national perspective. Michael Gerson in an article "An idea that should succeed in Washington," (7/9/2018) citing the need for prison and sentencing reform referenced two scholars, Steven Teles and David Dagan who identified reform as "an example of 'trans-partisanship," and "an agreement on policy goals driven by divergent, deeply held ideological beliefs." Everything depends on how people view crimes and criminals. They stated that "Liberals look at mass incarceration as see structural racism. Libertarians see the denial of civil liberties; Fiscal conservatives see wasted resources. Religious activists see inhumane conditions and damaged lives."

Gerson summed up the solution for mass incarceration, prison, and sentencing reform by making one simple statement - "All these convictions converge at one point: We should treat offenders as humans, with different stories and different needs, instead of casting them all into the same pit of despair." Easy to say, harder to accomplish.

Bigotry in Our Language is a Not So Hidden Secret We Can't Afford to Ignore

September 3, 2018

The objective from the very beginning was division and on a permanent basis as the reason the founding fathers invented two races, a black and a white. Unlike the Declaration of Independence and the U.S. Constitution that said we are one people, the concept of race has kept us separate and unequal. Subsequently, if we continue believing in the concept of races we will continue to be separate and never fulfill the objective of our democracy. If we are to ever have one nation, we will have to change the way to look, speak, and act towards one another. We also need to understand that the language we use helps to keep us separate. For example, if some people view themselves as black and white, they will not come together because of the historical significance of those words. They were meant to keep us apart.

Many well-meaning civic groups work against themselves by choosing a name that creates a negative and defensive feeling in others towards them. Take, for example, Black Lives Matter, a group that has an objective that is in keeping with the concept of democracy, but because of the word black in the name, it creates a defensive reaction in the minds of many European Americans.

We also have groups that use words like white, Aryan and Caucasian that they believe makes them different from people who do not look like them. Their pronounced goal is to save or preserve the so-call white race. They need to visit history to learn what happens to people who are separated or separate themselves from other people; they become extinct, like for example, the Australian Tasmanian Aboriginals, and in America, the Eire people and the colony of Roanoke.

When civic activists call for unity among people of color, they miss the opportunity to enhance their programs by not inviting all concerned people. Society have been conditioned to identify ourselves based on our so-called differences when our objective should be for all to use the same identity. We are all Americans, so why is it necessary to use color or ethnicity as part of identity? When visitors come to America, they come using their cultural identity. When Americans get a passport they provide a picture, but no racial or ethnic identity, because our cultural identity is American, not black or white, Hispanic or Asian etc.

We do ourselves a constant disservice by identifying ourselves as separate groups which have been our legacy since slavery. We have to grasp the reality of our situation understanding that the concept of biological races is a myth, invention, social construction, and lie. Prior to the Human Genome Project, everything about races with the numerous divisions, classifications, and characteristics was conjecture and opinion. We now have scientific proof, validation, and evidence that all human beings are more alike than penguins, and the skin complexion, eye shape and color, and hair texture are not unique to a select group of human beings. We are of one race of beings whether we like it or not.

We might think that language does not play so great a part in our lives and our behavior, but studies old and recent underscore the fact that when the words black and white are used in a sentence referring to an identity, a measured reaction occurs. The reaction for the European American, usually an increased heartbeat, is observed when the word black is used because of the social conditioning associated with the word. African Americans do not experience a similar reaction when the word white appeared in a sentence because they are conditioned to seeing it and without feeling threatened.

The media in American society contributes greatly to the separation of ethnic groups by the way they use inappropriate identity language. For example, if a bank is robbed and the robber was apprehended, nothing pertaining to the robbery is gained when the ethnicity of the robber is identified. Except, in American society today the identity of the robber is omitted if he or she happens to be European American, but the identity is almost always given when the robber's identity is a person of color. The effect of the naming the identity of the ethnic person serves to strengthen the negative stereotype society already has of the person of color.

Another way in which the media contributes to the negative stereotypes and biased attitudes held by some Americans relative to people of color has to do with the mentioning of the geographic location of an incident that is readily identified as being in a location where predominately people of color reside. Again, the mere mention of the location adds to the negative stereotype held by many people familiar with the location.

Today, with all the problems America is facing relative to our government and the various policies being addressed both positively and negatively, we need to take the opportunity to add our concept of race and identity into the mix and deal with it once and for all. We continue to talk about racism as if it was legitimate rather than bigotry which is what has been and continues to be practiced in society. Yes, our language uses the word racism to talk about social biases, but simultaneously serves to keep the concept of races alive and our society separate. We need to decide what kind of society we want to live in as well as our children and grandchildren. Once we make that choice, we need to get to work and make it happen. We have been talking about racism for three hundred years to no avail because we are still talking about it without a change in the daily behaviors of people. Racism is not the problem, we are because we refuse to accept the fact that we have been living in a false reality. What we cannot continue pretending to not see is the rapidly changing demographics that will force changes in society relative to cultural and ancestral identities.

We currently have an opportunity to make great strides in addressing our oneness as a society by debunking the myth of race and working to make America what it was meant to be a democracy. We will not and cannot get to where we want, and need, to be if we do not change from using our misleading ethnically biased language of bigotry.

Kaepernick's Protest is a Constitutional Exercise in American Democracy

August 31, 2016

Why are some people getting so bent out of shape over the fact that Colin Kaepernick decided to exercise his 1st Amendment right to protest what he sees as injustice in America? Ignorance of the Constitution? The excuse that Americans fought and died for our flag should not be used to justify complaints because all military takes an oath to uphold the Constitution, not the flag. The flag is only a symbol of the country and should be respected unless one wants to use it for protest, which is what Kaepernick has decided.

In America, if we have a problem with our government, we are taught to not run and hide, but to bring the problem out in the open so it can be addressed. The way the problem is brought to view is through protest. When the police or teachers reach an impasse in negotiations, they either chose a mediator or go on strike or both. Striking is a form of protest that has been used successfully for many years in America. None of the strikers have been accused of being unpatriotic or anti-American. They just want attention focused on their problem. Kaepernick is being patriotic by protesting in order to call attention to the problems he wants addressing.

Kaepernick is not the first athlete to protest by refusing to stand for the flag ceremony; nor will he be the last. His actions are not arbitrary or capricious, but well thought-out and reasoned. He knows that he will have to pay a price for his actions because too many people do not understand the thoughts that led to this action. In an article from the NFL Notes, Kaepernick is quoted as saying, "I'm going to continue to stand with the people that are being oppressed. …To me, this is something that has to change. When there's significant change and I feel like that flag represents what it's supposed to represent, this country is representing people the way that it's supposed to, I'll stand."

Regardless of how one feels about Kaepernick's form of protest, it should not be figured into the equation of right or wrong, because he is protesting as an American citizen. He is speaking out about the injustices visited upon African Americans and people of color in America. Other Americans see that same injustice but choose to remain silent. Why should Kaepernick be criticized for exercising his Constitutional right about injustices that have been going on for years while America looks on in silence? Some people believe that his decision to not stand for the flag is wrong, but that belief is theirs, and that is fine. What they do not have, however, is the right to select or judge Kaepernick's manner of protest. They might want to offer their opinion relative to what manner or form their protest would take, but no one can say whether their choice is right or wrong; it is theirs to make.

In America, citizens have for years refused to salute the flag, say the Pledge of Allegiance, and serve in the military. These people never receive complaints about their actions and are never accused of being un-American or unpatriotic; they are left alone to live their lives in a manner that suits them. Two groups of Americans in this category that come to mind are the Jehovah Witness and the Amish. In their defense, some people might call attention to their religious beliefs as reason enough for them to refuse to honor the flag or saying the Pledge and serving in the military. The irony of this defense is that they and Kaepernick use the same Constitutional rights to support their actions.

What some people do not like is for a person of notoriety to use his fame to call attention to his protest. To many people, a person gives up his right to be an individual to maintain his fame. With Kaepernick, some people want him to only be a football player, nothing more. If he says something that does not relate to football, he is criticizing for over-stepping his bounds. Many people want athletes to have no opinions outside of their sport. The fact that they are paid large sums of money to use their athletic abilities should be enough to keep them silent about other things. Unfortunately, that kind of thinking robs the individual of his whole being as an intelligent, sensible, and rational person capable of deciding apart from his professional career. We do not have to guess as to Kaepernick's motives for his protest, he stated that "No one's tried to quiet me and, to be honest, it's not something I'm going to be quite about…I'm going to speak the truth when I'm asked about it. This isn't for look. This isn't for publicity or anything like that. This is for people that don't have a voice. And this is for people that are being oppressed and need to have equal opportunities to be successful. To provide for families and not live in poor circumstances."

Many Americans apparently think that as Americans we should think and act in certain ways that do not offend the ideas or concepts they hold in high esteem. Were that the case, individual freedoms would be a laughing matter because they would not exist. As Americans, we are encouraged to believe that we can exercise our Constitutional rights without fear of anger, hate or some form of retribution for not walking in lock-step with what some people think is the right way.

Kaepernick did not call the media to witness him sitting during the flag ceremony; he did not seek to create a media storm that focused on his protest. The media took the lead in calling attention to the fact of Kaepernick's actions, and shortly afterward, judgments and criticisms flooded the airways. Whether one agrees with Kaepernick's form of protest, as Americans we must defend and support his rights to protest because that is what we believe is our responsibility. Let us be reminded of the importance of the right to be our individual selves by recalling the words of Henry David Thoreau: "If a man does not keep pace with his companions, perhaps it is because he hears a different drummer. Let him step to the music which he hears, however, measured or far away."

Removal of Symbols of Ethnic Bias Show Signs of Social Change

May 24, 2016

One of the general misconceptions many Americans have today is that ethnic prejudice is a thing of the past and only vestiges of it remain. For evidence of this social change some point to the removal of the Confederate flag from some Southern state flags as well as a number of statues and monuments that underscore the hatred and bigotry felt by many European Americans for African Americans during and after slavery. Another sign of attempts to remove symbols of ethnic bigotry on many college and university campuses is the removing of names of known bigots from buildings and other structures on the campus. For many institutions, this act of name removable represents a great and serious undertaking because many of those names belong to people who were considered deserving of the honor of recognition at the time they were displayed. What has changed to cause the removable of many of these former honored contributors from their place of recognition?

One answer can be found in history, but not necessarily the history written in school books; school book history was tailor-made to support the ethnic bigotry of the day. Much of the actual history resides in the old newspapers and journals of early America. What that history tells us is that ethnic bigotry was considered normal; to not be a bigot was considered not normal if one happened to be a European American (white). So, when people of the early American past were given honors via placing their names on buildings and other edifices, little attention was paid to or reference made to their ethnic bigotry. Such was apparently the case with the University of Tulsa naming one of its structures after John Rogers.

In an article in the *Oklahoman* (5/20/2016) "Building controversy provide cautionary tale," on the "Opinion" page, the writer tells about the removal of Roger's name from a TU building, not just any building: "University of Tulsa officials recently decided to remove John Roger's name from TU's college of law, which he helped found, because of his 1920s association with the Ku Klux Klan." The fact that the building was the college of law which Roger helped to found gives us some additional insight as to the mindset of the people of Oklahoma during this time. The article underscores the fact that "racists views of the Klan were not out of line with the thinking of many respectable people, across the nation, during Oklahoma's early decades." Few European Americans gave notice to the abuse, violence and death the Klan visited on African Americans. Since many of the up-standing, civic-minded, Christian, European American citizens were also Klan members, not many Oklahomans were told about the destruction and death caused by many of the good citizens of Tulsa in 1921 when the Greenwood area was demolished. The Klan has always stood for European American (white) supremacy and the inferiority of African Americans.

What we refer to today as a bigot was not considered bad or evil or even unpatriotic for early European Americans; as a matter of fact, the Klan for many European Americans was seen as an anti-crime, civic-minded, "temperance organization." Many of its members included bankers, businessmen, lawyers, educators, and even clergy. Helping to promote and maintain the Klan's views while passing them on to the children, were the text books. The article cited this reference: "Consider the 1914 biology textbook at the center of the famed Scopes 'monkey' trial in Tennessee. Based on evolutionary theory, that book matter-of-factly declared there were 'five races or varieties of man, … '"The article continued by listing the Ethiopian or Negro, the Malay or brown people, the American Indian, the Mongolians and finally, "the Caucasians represented by civilized white inhabitants of Europe and America."

The article underscored the importance of the text book: "That children's text book advocated eugenic, and said of supposedly inferior people, 'If such people were lower animals, we would probably kill them off to prevent them from spreading." Such was the mindset of many of the European American Oklahomans in the early 1920s according to the article. However, in another article in the *Oklahoman* (5/6/2016) 'These were everywhere,' tells of the many Klan klaverns in Oklahoma before and during the 1940s. This article tells some of the Klan's activities as in the following reference: "A story in the Nov. 21, 1920, edition of *The Daily Oklahoman* describes Klansmen terrorizing residents in Guthrie, threatening farmers, business owners and residents in the city's black quarter with death." Also, it included: "According to the story, the Klan forbid cotton growers from paying pickers more than $1.25 per hundred pounds picked, and blacks were threatened with death and burning if they asked for a higher wage."

The Klan article showed a map of Klan chapters in Oklahoma in the early 1940—it was home to 102 chapters. The article concluded with the findings that "The Southern Poverty Law Center recognized 10 Klan-affiliated groups last year in Oklahoma." Although laws have changed over the years, many attitudes and minds still embrace the once normal bigoted psyche. The lingering hate and fear of African Americans in some Oklahomans might easily be assumed from the fact that all seventy-seven counties voted against Barack Obama two times—2008 and 2012. Obama was not liked by many European Americans before he had a chance to assume his office; the reason given for his unpopularity was not his skin color but his political party.

We can certainly applaud the efforts of the University Tulsa to remove symbolic references to our biased past and support them in their actions. We can also applaud the efforts of the *Oklahoman's* article discussing the removal of John Roger's name from TU's law college and shedding some light on why the removal is important. One of the most challenging aspects of American society today is to understand that because the normal mindset of European Americans is biased towards African Americans and other people of color, "basic morality and common sense" must be redefined without the bias. For us to assume that ethnic bigotry simply fades away into the woodwork over time would be wrong; removing it takes great effort mainly because many people do not realize they are biased.

Charlottesville, a Sign of the Changing Times of Bigotry in America

August 13, 2017

The social unrest taking place in Charlottesville, Virginia involving the extremist right-wing groups is an indication of at least two things: one, their march was organized to show society the large number of people belonging to and supporting their cause; two, although this was not an objective of the activity, it showed the fear and anxiety of the social changes taking place in society today, and their desire to stop or slow down those changes.

The lie that the founding fathers invented concerning the concept of a black race and a white race and the institution of a system of white supremacy has finally shown signs of deconstruction. As long as the Anglo-Saxons in America were in control of society, they could manage the bigoted social atmosphere. Many European Americans today do not realize the fact that they are bigots because they were conditioned to view bigotry as natural. Everywhere a European American looked in society, they saw people who looked like them always in control. All the social institutions, including the media, constantly underscored the values and standard embodied and promoted by the European Americans. So, they naturally saw themselves as superior to all others who did not reflect their image.

European Americans were so deceived by their skin color that they believed their good will and charity toward people of color and lesser whites would serve to attest to their goodness and Christian virtues while not realizing that the mere fact of viewing another human being as inferior to them or not deserving of respect and dignity was a disservice to humanity and a slap in the face of their god. The fact that the Bible and science have underscored countless times the existence of one race seem to have no effect on their sense of reality because they are constantly reminded that their skin color gives them supremacy. They prefer to hold on to a lie rather than embrace the truth.

Since the American government embraced the concept of bigotry based on skin color and has never sought to correct the lie, they share part of the responsibility for the civil unrest in Charlottesville. Their responsibility rest upon the fact that groups of people believe in the myth of a white race and the government not stopping to correct them, allows them to proceed as though their actions are acceptable. The right-wing extremist groups base their existence on the false concept of a so-called white race. Their objectives are to preserve and promote their conception of their white race, and the government simply tells them not to break any laws while pretending to be white. The time has come for the government and society to give power to the truth—we are all part of the human family regardless of our skin color.

Some of the facts that the government does not want to be communicated is that African Americans and non-Anglo-Saxon peoples were never intended to become citizens of America, and now that they are citizens, they must be constantly exploited socially and economically. African Americans were never freed from slavery; their enslavement simply took other forms that prevented them from gaining a foothold on which to build a successful life. Those forms included segregation, discrimination, bigotry, less than standard (their standards) schools, jobs, economic and political power.

What the founding fathers never thought would happen, happened— an African American was elected to the Presidency of the United States of America. This phenomenon occurrence caused a shock wave throughout the country, but especially in the seat of government, Washington D.C. where some of the Republican politicians felt a sense of fear and dread. A plan to counter the new state of affairs was set in motion to deny the new president everything possible.

What the extremists marching in Charlottesville realize is that their sense of importance and power based on their skin complexion is rapidly diminishing, so they must use every tool available to them to try to prevent that loss from happening. Many of these extremists discovered that there were many Americans who believed as they did but were not willing to expose themselves publicly. Some use the political arena to try to meet their objectives by creating laws that seek to undo many of the social and political gains experienced by people of color. Many of the bigots believe they have support from the current President of the United States and seek to express their sense of power in ways that do not incur serious repercussions. Reference to law enforcement's treatment of people of color is one example of how bigotry is being expressed today.

The confrontation of extremist groups and other citizens should come as no surprise since we all know that change for the bigots is devastating and final. Today we witness many injustices committed against people of color by bigots who are protected by law and numbers in power. However, one thing is certain, change is happening; America is browning and the number of people of color will eventually be the majority population. The power will change hands and if we want a society that treats all its citizens justly and fairly, we must start working on those changes now. The battle being fought by the extremists today are being waged in ignorance that continues to be conditioned by society and the lie of race.

America is going through a series of important changes that will affect how we look at ourselves as a society and how the world sees us. Too often we look at other countries and cultures and make judgment statements based on our limited knowledge of history, our and the worlds while failing to recognize that other countries are also looking at us and judging us by our words and actions. Common sense and the truth can serve as a beginning towards building the kind of society we want our children and grandchildren to live in, a society that does not judge a people by the color of their skin, but the measure of their character.

Five questions that can aid in reducing arrest of people of color due to 911 calls

November 21, 2018

Although they occur with too much frequency, we must not let the incidents of police arrest of people of color and other poor citizens for being in a place that appears uncomfortable to some European Americans become acceptable and ordinary. What seems like a daily occurrence of a person being arrested by the police in response to a 911 call must be addressed and corrected. In <u>order</u> to make the corrections three areas must be targeted: the citizen who makes the 911 call, the 911 dispatcher, and the police officers who respond to the 911 call.

Individuals that serve in any of the three above capacities must be taught that their choices can and often make the difference between a person's life and death. Therefore, before the choice to act or react relative to a 911 call the following questions should be addressed: who, what, where, when, and why. If the small amount of time it takes to consider these questions by individuals in each of three areas of concern, society would benefit greatly with fewer arrest, fewer deaths, and less <u>money</u> paid by the citizens to settle civil cases. These questions should accompany any orientation relative to the service of a 911 emergency call because they provide the necessary information from which to make a reasonable and rational decision and choice relative to a perceived emergency.

Any number of reasons can be recalled for why a European American citizen calls 911 for assistance. For example, a university professor from the University of Texas in San Antonio called 911 to have a student remove from class because the student had simply placed her feet in or on the chair in front of her. Prior to making the call, if the professor had taken the time to ask herself the question why she wanted the student removed, the subsequent action that took place might not have happened. We might assume from the report that followed the <u>incident</u> that the professor felt that the gesture by the student was interpreted as an insult to her. The student's actions were not based on anything having to do with the teacher; she just simply wanted to stretch her legs. Unfortunately, the police arrived and escorted the student from the classroom. We might add that the student was an African American and was simply unaware of the professor's thoughts and reactions, but had to bear the brunt of the incident by being removed from the class. The information derived from asking the five questions could have offered a remedy for the problem.

Too often the 911 caller is in an emotional state of mind and cannot reason or adequately address the situation that is thought to require a 911 call. In that case, the 911 dispatcher should try to obtain that information before it is dispatched to officers in the field. In any number of incidents, a little time and a little more information might have prevented the need for law enforcement assistance. If we were to examine the situation that occurred at a Starbuck's restaurant involving two young African Americans waiting on another colleague to <u>join</u> them being arrested and escorted out of the establishment by the police, we realize that simply answering the five questions might have eliminated the need for law enforcers. Had the dispatcher taken the time to ascertain just what was the problem involving the African Americans before contacting the police, the incident might have been avoided. However, the social conditioning of many European Americans often causes them to react in fear or dread at the mention of or sight of a person of color in the near surroundings, so the first reaction is to call 911.

When police receive information from a 911 dispatcher, they usually react based on the information they receive. One serious problem generally associated with this action has to be with the education the police receive in the orientation to the job and its responsibilities, namely, attitude and judgment towards the citizens. We know from many studies and experiences that European American law enforcers have a different emotional reaction to incidents involving African Americans and European Americans. Too often the attitude of officers toward people of color is one of fear, dread, and guilt. In essence, too often people of color are viewed and treated as criminals before any questions are asked or additional information acquired beyond what the dispatcher offered.

For example, when a convenience store employee thought a young African American <u>college student</u> had used a fake $20 bill to pay for his merchandise, he immediately called 911. The dispatcher relayed the information to the police and they rushed to the store. When they arrive inside the store, they went immediately to the African American student and commanded him to show an identification card. Nothing was said to him prior to this command. Based on their action, they assumed that the student was a criminal as in this case; the officers thought the student was not producing his identification fast enough so they ordered him to place his hands behind him, and thus instigated what they describe as the need for physical force. After throwing the student to the floor, shocking him, and placing him in handcuffs, the officers asked the store employees for the fake $20 dollar bill only to discover that it was nowhere to be found. The student was taken to jail for not obeying a direct command.

When we look at the actions and reactions of the three areas of concern relative to some European American citizens calling 911, the actions of the 911 dispatcher, and finally, the involvement of the police in these incidents, we can certainly justify the need for the use of the five questions along the chain of information from the caller to the police officers. As citizens, we pay for and depend on the services of the dispatches and the police officers to do their jobs, and we should also expect them to show respect and courtesy to everyone without first prejudging them.

Replacing the Concept of Race with Reality in Five Extremely Challenging and Life-Changing Steps

November 28, 2018

Although it might seem strange today, people initially thought that the earth was flat, and not a sphere. Around the year 500 A.D., a Greek named Pythagoras introduced the concept of the earth being a sphere, but people paid little notice until Aristotle, some two-hundred years later, 330 A.D., promoted the same concept. People were not eager to give up the concept of a flat earth. Even places in the Christian Bible show evidence of the concept of the earth being flat. Eventually, the voyages of Christopher Columbus and Ferdinand Magellan among others provided proof of the planet is a sphere. The acceptance of this fact brought with it a necessary change in the way earth was viewed. The concept of the flat earth was not destroyed or changed; it was replaced with scientific facts.

The point of the concept of a flat earth being replaced by the concept of a round one underscored the importance of fact and evidence in the process. Today, we have a similar situation before us with respect to the concept of race by color or geography that no longer has rational or realistic basics. Replacing this concept of race is extremely challenging because of the rewards associated with the identity of one group—European

Americans. The problem exists because America's Founding father invented and instituted a system of a race by color with two colors, black and white, playing major roles. Society was conditioned and forced to view the Anglo-Saxons (whites) as superior to all other races regardless of color, but especially the people of African descent. The concept of race by color became over several hundred years to be accepted as normal although it was constantly challenged because of its basic flaws.

Nevertheless, people of all persuasions accepted the concept and wrote about it like it was valid and factual. At one point in 1883, the term eugenics was coined by a British scientist who led the attempt to develop a super race. Fortunately, those efforts failed, but the studies continued until today the results of a study, the Human Genome Project, involving DNA revealed that all human beings are 99.09% alike. Many people do not want to accept the scientific evidence that proved the concept of race by color to be bogus. So, how does one go about replacing the concept of race by color to one of reality?

The very first step is to recognize that the concept of race by color is a myth, that all human beings belong to the same race; that all human being are a shade of brown, not black and white; that intelligence and character cannot be based on skin color. Because most, if not all of these things, have been a part of the national conscientiousness for centuries, recognizing them as false cannot happen easily. For some people, it is asking too much regardless of the facts and evidence that view race as not factual or valid. All people must be seen and accepted as part of the human family without anyone ethnic group being superior or inferior to any other.

The second step is to accept the fact that all Americans have been socially conditioned to accept the concept of race by color as normal and natural and before any positive progress can be made, this concept must be rejected and replaced with factual truths. This second step is extremely difficult because while some Americans can see prejudice and bigotry in others, they cannot or do not see it in themselves. That is why the first step is necessary. People who refer to themselves or others as black or white do not realize that in using those terms they are connecting with the past and the concept of race by color. The concept of race has to be replaced with ethnic group or ethnicity in order to not get caught in the trap seeing race by color. The identity of European Americans can no longer include the color white because white is simply the adjective preceding the noun race.

The third step involves a commitment to promote the concept of the human family that includes all ethnic groups, including European Americans as a part of that family. In other words, we recognize, respect and accept Americans with cultural differences from our own. We realize that just because our ethnic identity is different from some other ethnic group that does not give us the right to treat them differently and judges them as not being our equals. If we are all Americans, then everyone should expect and receive fairness and legal justice before the law. Unfortunately, America has not conditioned us to think and act that way. So, the commitment includes recognizing and working towards correcting the problems created by the concept of race by color. For example, the problem of voting rights, the problem of incarceration of the poor, the problem of substandard schools, the problem substandard housing, the problem of low paying jobs, the problem of law enforcement 's bias against people of color. In other words, working towards correcting problems that affect all Americans, but that has been aimed primarily at the poor and people of color.

The fourth step involves a degree of self-discipline that keeps us from losing focus on our objective—replacing the concept of race. We have all been conditioned by our society, and especially by our concept and interpretation of our history. Our demographics are rapidly changing and having a great impact on society, so we need to remember America's mantra: "e Pluribus Unum"—from many one. Unity must be our focus and objective.

The fifth step is the need to recognize and accept consistency in our thoughts and actions. Replacing the conception of race from what we were conditioned to believe to the reality of what we face in society today is a tremendous undertaking. When Joseph J. Ellis, a best-selling historian was asked the question: "What is the biggest failing of the Founders that still haunts us today?" He answered that "When the Founders talked about 'we the people,' they were not talking about black people. They weren't talking about women, and they weren't talking about Native Americans. Whenever race enters the question, the Founders are going to end up disappointing you."

Replacing race with reality –an acceptance of all human beings as a family that is based on facts is the way society will move into a positive future.

Afterword

The blog selections in this book represent an attempt to show how the concept of race and bigotry, part of our American social conditioning have played and continues to play a part in our daily lives. The objective for presenting these examples is to underscore the fact that the bigotry and biases by European Americans against primarily people of color are based purely on a false concept of so-called racial superiority. This concept of superiority was the invention of the Founding Fathers and was based on defining race by skin color—black and white. Since race cannot be determined or defined by skin color the concept of superiority could be sustained only as long as the proponents of that concept controlled society through laws and behavior. What many of these selections show is the fact that many European Americans never realized that their perception of themselves and that of others was biased. The reality of that superior belief is time and time again seen in the power, privilege, and arrogance displayed by European Americans known as white privilege.

European Americans have been conditioned to believe that they are the center of the universe and every thing they say and do is normal and correct and protected by their skin color and identity. As stated earlier, that belief was based on a false premise and is presently being debunked at a rapid social pace. Coming to grips with the truth of the concept of ethnic superiority is extremely challenging for many European Americans as well as to some people of color. However, the evidence supporting the falseness of the race concept has become more than sufficient to dispute the claim. None-the-less, when a reference is made to the bigotry in American being a part of the social fabric some people are quick to defend the status quo as being democratic with liberty and justice for all.

The facts are that at the end of the Civil War the former slaves were set free with nothing but what they could carry with them. No, they did not receive forty acres and a mule when the war ended in 1865. However, in 1889 the government declared some unassigned land in Oklahoma open for the taking. Sam Anderson in his book, Boom *Town*, noted that "The Land Run was for white men. Not officially, in a legal sense, but in practice. The number of African Americans who made the Run is, like many things about that day, hard to pin down, but at least one historian guesses it was fewer than fifty." Anderson mentioned the opportunity that acquiring land meant for poor and isolated people and that their absence in the Run spoke for itself. He noted that "Oklahoma settlers were a heavily armed white mob. Black American would have known to proceed with caution."

Many of the incidents discussed in the blog selections deal with some European Americans who have no idea that their actions and behavior demonstrate a form of bigotry and sense of white privilege. The lack of awareness of an ethnic bias would not be due to a lack of examples which occur daily. That bigotry was in fact a part of the mind-set of European Americans and that it was undemocratic was evident in the comments of one of the early founders of Oklahoma City, Angel Scott, as Anderson noted "I always treated them as human beings, and always hated with all my soul the poisonous attitude of so many so-called Christian people of Oklahoma against their race." So, the claim of innocence of ethnic bigotry is difficult to accept from European Americans today.

The blog selections are not offered to cause discontent and guilt to the readers who might experience them because of the bigotry represented in them, but to show that with some reason and common sense many of the incidents would have not occurred or been the subject of attention. Each of the selection conclude with some positive element that gives hope for a better tomorrow through our efforts. Because when we know better, we do better.